Humanity must perforce prey on itself,
like monsters of the deep.

King Lear

THE AGE OF TORQUEMADA

by

John E. Longhurst

CORONADO PRESS

Lawrence, Kansas, U.S.A.

Second Edition, 1964

Copyright 1962

by

Coronado Press
Box 3232
Lawrence, Kansas 66044

Third Printing
March, 1973

Manufactured in the U.S.A.

ILLUSTRATIONS

The Jews of Cologne are burnt alive	5
Jews taking the blood from Christian children	16
The ritual murder of Simon of Trent	26
The reign of Antichrist	53
The Castle of Triana, headquarters of the Inquisition	70
El Greco's "The Inquisitor General"	74
The water torture	100

CONTENTS

Introduction	xi
I THE CHOSEN PEOPLE	3
II THE GOLDEN AGE	19
III 1391	31
IV THE CONVERSO	45
V TRAITORS TO THE FAITH	55
VI THE INQUISITION	64
VII INQUISITOR GENERAL TORQUEMADA	73
VIII THE ALBORAICO	83
IX DENUNCIATION FOR SURVIVAL	96
X THE REMNANT	110
XI THE RITUAL MURDER OF LA GUARDIA	118
XII THE WANDERING JEW	129
XIII THE MESSIAH COMETH	138

Introduction

THERE IS A STAGGERING BODY OF LITERATURE on the subjects of Judaism and the Spanish Inquisition, in both secondary and primary sources. For the Jews, the most useful works are those of Heinrich Graetz, Cecil Roth, Joseph Jacobs, Abraham Neuman, José Amador de los Ríos, and Nicolás López Martínez. Facts and fancy about the early years of the Inquisition may be found in the writings of Henry C. Lea, Juan Antonio Llorente, Julio Melgares Marín, Francisco Javier García Rodrigo, Miguel de la Pinta Llorente, and Bernardino Llorca, among many others.

For the writings of contemporaries of the events described here, one may examine the many published chronicles of the fifteenth and early sixteenth centuries which are listed in abundance in Sánchez Alonso's *Fuentes para la historia de España e Hispanoamérica*. The most important primary materials, however, are the documents themselves. Many of them have been printed, both with and without comment, by Jewish and Spanish scholars of the nineteenth century in three learned journals: *Sefarad,* the *Revue des études Juives,* and the *Boletín de la Real Academia de la historia*. The latter is perhaps the most valuable of all, due primarily to the tireless and meticulous labors of the Spanish Jesuit investigator, Fidel Fita. More recently, the German scholar Fritz Baer has published two massive volumes of documents (Berlin, 1926–1936), under the title *Die Juden im Christlichen Spanien*. He has included in this project—either in full or in abstract—the extant documentary material on Spanish Jewry from the Middle Ages to the year of the expulsion, with a few additional items on the immediate after-effects, from which the final chapter of the present study has been prepared.

I have read many of the original trials of the early Inquisition years, which are housed in the *Archivo Histórico Nacional* in Madrid, and it has also been my good fortune to go through the original papers in the Henry C. Lea collection at the University of

Pennsylvania, which contains much useful material from which Mr. Lea drew for his studies on the Spanish Inquisition.

There is, however, no simple correlation between the extent of one's investigations and his "objectivity" when writing about a subject like the Spanish Inquisition. All the literature on this topic, including the present work, is charged with the personal views of its authors. It is all, therefore, "partisan" or "subjective," although it may vary in reliability according to the authors' use of documentary sources and their sense of historical rectitude. I have no desire to single out any particular class, unless they single themselves out first for special consideration, and it appears to me that three modern Spanish authors have done this. Nicolás López Martínez, Bernardino Llorca, and Miguel de la Pinta Llorente, who are understandably "reasonable" about the Inquisition, are all careful investigators whose historical methods of research are above reproach. They insist, however, that because they work from documents, their viewpoints and conclusions are as "objective" and "unprejudiced" as their methodology. They likewise insist that all other historians who see things differently from themselves are "biased" and "prejudiced" and cannot be relied upon. The fact remains that other historians besides our three Spanish colleagues are quite as conscientious and capable in matters of methodology, and are every bit as trustworthy. Both "sides" operate within the framework of certain values and ideals: the judgments of Henry C. Lea, for example, are quite apparent, and he makes no pretence about his feelings. Less overt, perhaps, but equally apparent nonetheless, are the preconceptions of his critics. The latter's preemption of the ritualism of "objectivity" and "impartiality" puts one in mind of Shakespeare's observation about people who protest too much. The only advice I can give to the student of this subject is to be alert to the predispositions of all of us, especially when we suggest that we alone have the Truth.

THE
AGE OF
TORQUEMADA

CHAPTER 1

The Chosen People

THE JEWS HAVE BEEN HISTORICALLY USEFUL to Western man, providing him with a handy vehicle for hooliganism, statecraft, and righteous orthodoxy against the race of Antichrist. Europe's Jews in the early Middle Ages were relatively better off than in other periods—before and since—and suffered only spasmodic frenzies of persecution which, being capricious rather than calculated, died out as quickly as they had begun. Although Jews were shunned by Christians as dabblers in the black arts and assassins of the Redeemer, they were generally left to their own devices such as moneylending, an occupation forbidden to Christians as Scripturally unjustifiable.

Unfortunately for the Jews, however, in the latter half of the eleventh century, infidel hordes from hither Asia began pressing hard on the flanks of Eastern Europe. By 1096 these descendants of Attila, known as Seljuk Turks, had overrun all of Asia Minor, threatening at any moment to burst into Europe itself. Worst of all, they had seized the Holy City of Jerusalem, polluting the Purple Blood of the Lamb with their unclean Mohammedan abominations, as Western holy men liked to put it. West Europeans responded to the Saracen threat with a series of military expeditions to the East which ultimately came to be known to Christian posterity as the Crusades to the Holy Land.

To stimulate enthusiasm for the Crusades, preaching friars, hermits, and other persons of undoubted sanctity travelled about Europe enumerating the virtues of exterminating the Infidel and exhorting the Faithful to take up arms against the Saracen host. The precarious toleration accorded the Jews in Europe quickly dissolved in the universal excitement created by the prospect of a Holy War. If it was a pious necessity to destroy infidels in the deserts of Asia, why should they be permitted to blaspheme the Savior at home? Peter the "Venerable," abbot of the great French monastery at Cluny, in urging Louis VII of France to undertake the second crusade, spoke for a whole generation:

> *Of what use is it,* (he wrote) *to go forth to seek the enemies of Christendom in different lands, if the blasphemous Jews, who are much worse than the Saracens, are permitted in our very midst to scoff with impunity at Christ and the sacrament! The Saracen at least believes as we do that Christ was born of a virgin, and yet he is execrable, since he denies the incarnation. How much more these Jews who disbelieve everything, and mock at everything! Yet I do not require you to put to death these accursed beings, because it is written, "Do not slay them." God does not wish to annihilate them, but like Cain, the fratricide, they must be made to suffer fearful torments, and be preserved for greater ignominy, for an existence more bitter than death. They are dependent, miserable and terror-stricken, and must remain in that state until they are converted to the Savior. You ought not to kill them, but to afflict them in a manner befitting their baseness.*

If God had no desire to annihilate the Jews, as the Venerable Peter said, some of His flock did. The two centuries of the Crusades against the Saracens of Asia were paralleled by continuing massacres of the Jews of Europe. In the very first year of the Holy Wars, hordes of self-styled crusaders in Germany began the work of purification by wiping out the Jewish communities of

THE CHOSEN PEOPLE

THE JEWS OF COLOGNE ARE BURNT ALIVE. (From a 15th century woodcut.)

Treves, Speyer, Worms, Mainz, and Cologne. In two months some twelve thousand Jews are estimated to have been killed, while thousands of others saved themselves by accepting Christian baptism.

Crusaders from all countries soon caught the fever and warmed up for the Saracens by destroying Jewish communities in the path of their march eastward. The Jews back home fared no better. A body of crusaders assembled in Aquitania attacked a number of Jewish communities throughout southern France, offering their inhabitants the alternatives of Christian baptism or infidel death. When the bulk of the Jews rejected the Cross, the crusaders trampled them beneath the hoofs of their horses, a popular method used against the Saracens in the Holy Land. Then they burned down the Jews' houses and built great bonfires with their sacred books. During one wild summer, some three thousand Jews perished in southern France, and five hundred were "converted" to Christianity.

In England the Jews were relatively undisturbed until the Lion-Hearted crusader, Richard I, ascended the throne in 1189. On the day of Richard's coronation, the London mob celebrated by looting and burning Jewish homes, murdering their inhabitants, and sacking the London synagogue. The following year, while Richard was chasing infidels in Asia, his subjects were rooting them out at home. Mobs attacked the Jewish communities in several English towns, the greatest violence taking place at York. There the terrified Jews held out for six days against a beseiging army of rabble, sometime crusaders, and clergy. When all hope of resistance was gone they slew one another to avoid falling into the hands of the Faithful.

In the years which followed, public massacres in England increased in fury. Fifteen hundred Jews were killed during the celebration of Easter Week in London. In Northampton a rumor that the Jews there had crucified a Christian child brought bloody retribution when a number of suspects were torn apart by horses and their remains distributed about the town square. Meanwhile, Parliament was grinding out new restrictions against the Jews and the Crown was prying money from them for "reasons of state," which led a contemporary cynic to observe that the Jews of England were being treated like their ancestors in Egypt, except that they were required to furnish gold instead of bricks. The end finally came in 1290 when Edward I expelled all Jews from the realm. The edict of expulsion met with popular approval, and certainly won the admiration of the Italian bankers who replaced the Jews as moneylenders to the English Crown.

The French seemed to have trouble making up their minds about expelling the Jews of that country. A royal edict of 1181 banned all Jews from Paris and its environs. The Hebrew problem still plagued the rest of the country however. A few years after the purging of Paris, King Philip Augustus had to burn upwards of a hundred Jews at the town of Bray because, rumor had it, they had avenged themselves on a man who murdered a Jew by crowning the culprit with thorns and then hanging him. The

Jews were expelled from all of France in 1306, but the law was not strictly enforced and was rescinded nine years later. Soon after that, the French Jews were caught up in one of those spontaneous "crusades" which had lately been flaring up among the rustics of Western Europe. On this particular occasion, a band of forty thousand sheepherders, led by a local prophet whose heavenly visions guaranteed him and his followers sure victory over the Saracens, decided to get in some practice against their Jewish neighbors before embarking for the Holy Land. They marched through France, a swarm of avenging angels in buckskin and pitchfork, burning and killing as they went. At Verdun, where some five hundred Jews took refuge in the city's fortress, the sheepmen-crusaders stormed the tower and slaughtered all those who had not wisely committed suicide. Similar massacres followed in Bordeaux, Gascogne, Toulouse, and other towns in the south of France. Before this preliminary crusade was over, more than one hundred and twenty Jewish congregations had been destroyed.

Whereas England and France had some semblance of national organization in the person of the Crown, Germany in the Middle Ages was a disorganized political hodge-podge of several hundred petty feudal principalities and independent towns. Consequently the persecutions there lacked overall direction or sanction, and varied with the moods and circumstances of local governments. But what the Germans lacked in organization they made up for in enthusiasm. The domestic battalions of the third crusade, made up mostly of God-fearing peasants, marched on Jewish communities from the Rhine River all the way to Vienna. Some years later, during a disorderly interval between the death of one German emperor and the disputed election of his successor, Jews were slain by the thousands in Coblenz, Erfurt and Sinzig. In the latter city all the members of the congregation were burned alive while celebrating the Sabbath in the synagogue, and public-spirited citizens assumed the title of "Judenbreter" ("Jew-Roaster"), vying with one another over the number of Jews they had ignited with their own hands.

At Rottingen, in Franconia, the natives were stirred by the appearance in their midst of a Jew-killer named Rindfleisch. Like others of his breed, he had received an appointment from Heaven to wipe out the accursed race of Moses. It did not take him long to recruit an army of crusaders among the good folk of Rottingen, which began its work by rounding up all the Jews in town and setting fire to them. From Rottingen the crusaders marched on other towns in need of cleansing, the ranks of their army growing constantly. Everywhere they went the most exciting slaughter followed. The Jewish quarter at Wurzburg, which had pulled itself together again after being worked over by earlier crusaders, was this time destroyed for good. At Nuremberg, where the Jews took refuge in the town fortress, their resistance was overcome in a series of bloody assaults and they were all butchered on the spot. Elsewhere in Germany other inspired leaders operating under celestial orders led armies of holy avengers throughout Bavaria and into Austria. For seven months the orgy continued. By the time it spent itself, more than one hundred and forty Jewish congregations, comprising one hundred thousand persons, had been swept away.

When the Crusades were over and the enthusiasm for killing infidels had been dissipated by the attractions of a revived trade and commerce, a new disaster fell upon the Jews. Trading ships from the East, infested by rats, brought with them the terrible Black Death. Within two years (1348–1349) bubonic plague carried off one fourth of the people of Western Europe and so dislocated every phase of life that it even forced the French and English to settle for a temporary peace in their dreary Hundred Years War.

As the number of deaths grew, it became increasingly obvious that the plague was a diabolical Jewish plot to wipe out the entire Christian population of the West. Confessions wrung from a handful of Jewish "conspirators" on the torture racks at Geneva verified the general conviction: the Black Death had originated with the Jews of Spain, who had a deep knowledge of the occult arts. In Toledo, the center of Jewish learning, specialists in black magic were brewing poisons made from spiders, frogs and lizards, or as some of the more sophisticated versions had it, from the hearts of Christians combined with the dough of consecrated Communion wafers. From there the poison was shipped to Jews all over Europe, convoyed by secret agents bearing instructions for its most effective use. Local Jews, skulking about in the dead of night, poured the poison into rivers, brooks and wells from which Christians obtained their water.

The best therapy for the Black Death, therefore, was to kill Jews. The results were so appalling that one's sense of the awful character of the horrors which followed is blunted by their sheer quantity. A few samples will suffice. In numerous cities the entire Jewish congregations of men, women and children were burned alive. The city fathers of Basle built a large house on an island in the Rhine, herded all the local Jews into it and burned it down to the ground. Four hundred Jews at Worms, and two thousand at Strassburg, died in the flames. The Jewish colonies of Oppenheim and Frankfurt committed mass suicide to escape their enemies. Rioting mobs in Mainz stoned, pummelled and stamped to death nearly six thousand Jews. In Vienna all the members of the congregation killed themselves in the synagogue. Before the Black Death had passed, the same drama had worked out to the same disgraceful climax all over Europe.

A popular accompaniment to these orgies of persecution was the growth of the legend of the Jewish Ritual Murder. The modern psychoanalyst, probing into the dark corners of the mind, might cast some light on the origins of such legends as this one. Our own lack of sophistication in the subtleties of psychological investigation, however, restricts us to more commonplace speculations. In the historical memory of the race, there were in the Middle Ages (and still are today) certain residual impressions of barbaric rituals from the ancient past. Such rituals had their "practical" purpose: to placate the gods, to wheedle some special favor from them, or to fortify oneself against present and future dangers from a capricious Mother Nature or hostile demons. With the advance of civilization and the apparent desire for more socially acceptable methods to achieve the same ends, the ancient practices were discarded in favor of less strenuous pastimes like knocking on wood and dancing around a maypole. Nonetheless, the memories of ancient science were still strong in the Middle Ages, and while no respectable person practiced such things, respectable people attributed them to their enemies. The Jewish Ritual Murder, which is one illustration of this habit, is an interesting compound of several elements of savage practices from the dim past.

Human sacrifice was an almost universal custom in early times. Adult victims, especially criminals and prisoners of war, were sometimes used, but children were more popular. Young maidens were the special favorites of unfriendly dragons, while little boys were useful for a wide variety of purposes. In ancient Greece the kings of Thessaly sacrificed their first son to Zeus. Their Hebrew counterparts, according to Philo of Byblus, sacrificed their sons in times of danger to propitiate the avenging demons. The Old Testament relates how King Mesha of Moab effected the withdrawal of a besieging army of Israelites by delivering up his son as a burnt offering on the town walls. Abraham was on the point of sacrificing his only son Isaac when an Angel of the Lord stayed his upraised knife at the last moment. A legendary king of Sweden sought immortality by offering his nine sons to Odin in exchange for a little more time, and in medieval Europe everybody knew that witches improved their own standing with the Prince of Darkness by the ritual sacrifice of unbaptized children.

Another element in the Jewish Ritual Murder legend is the use of a substitute when the original object of interest is unavailable. One of the most common of all superstitions was that a man could be injured through his footprints. History is full of examples of vengeful aborigines piercing an enemy's footprints with spears, while their medieval cousins preferred to hammer nails in them. And everybody has heard of the modern voodoo festivals in Haiti where native witches can kill a man by abusing his effigy in doll size. Different problems call for different solutions: an exciting variation of this theme of magical sympathy calls for the use of a live human being in place of the god. This was once a common practice in the Eastern Mediterranean and also in Mexico, where the Aztecs annually sacrificed a young man in the role of the god Tezcatlipoca.

The human heart has always enjoyed a special cult of its own as the seat and symbol of life. Before the white men came to domesticate them, the Indians of the New World used to cut out their victims' hearts and offer them to the sun god to build up his energy for the long trip across the heavens. A more selfish motive prompted the ancients to eat the heart of a valiant enemy to acquire his powers for themselves. This seems almost finicky in comparison with the modern "Leopard Man" of the Cameroons, who eats the whole body, including the heart and all the other internal machinery. But this is too gross to interest anyone except the sensual dullard and the anthropologist. Other examples are more imaginative: Arab chroniclers of the ninth century tell of a man-tiger named Ibrahim ibn Ahmed, Prince of Sicily and North Africa, who confounded his enemies by cutting out their hearts and weaving them into a garland with which to festoon the gates of Tunis.

Blood also has a special fascination for the practitioner of the occult arts. Babylonian legend tells of Lilith the "night-monster" who had a special power of evil over children. In the Rabbinical literature of the Jews, she became the first wife of Adam but left him to become queen of the succubi and suck the blood of infants. Blood had its practical uses as well as its pleasures. The Gauls of the early Middle Ages drank the blood of an enemy to inherit his strength. In Peru the Incas kneaded maize with human blood to make a paste which they rubbed on their bodies to protect them from disease. Early Christian writings relate how the Faithful rushed into the arena to smear themselves with a protective coating of the blood of their martyred colleagues. Cotton Mather spoke of "getting the Blood of the Great Passover sprinkled on our houses" to stop an epidemic of measles in Boston in 1713, and in 1890 a Galician magician was convicted of stealing the corpses of two Jewish children and sprinkling their blood to sterilize a house infected with typhoid.

If we place these residual recollections against the prevailing superstitions of the Middle Ages, the Jewish Ritual Murder fits perfectly into a popular system of insane logic. For this was a world in which the invisible was terrifyingly real—a world where witches sailed across the sky on broomsticks, warlocks destroyed innocent babies in the womb, incubi and succubi lay with unsuspecting humans to propagate the infernal race of demons, and agents of the Devil swarmed around the dying to snatch their souls to Hell. If we add to all this the hot conviction that the Jew was a Doctor of the Black Arts, the sworn enemy of all Christians and, indeed, the Antichrist himself, then we have all the necessary ingredients for concocting the myth of the Jewish Ritual Murder.

The favorite sport of the Jews, as medieval gossip had it, was to torture and crucify a Christian boy in celebration of the Passover, which generally coincided with the Christian Easter. These stories started, naturally enough, with the launching of the Crusades, although it was almost fifty years before the first case of a Jewish Ritual Murder was formally recorded in the "history" books for transmission to a credulous posterity.[1] On Easter eve

---

[1] They are still being recorded in our own day. Waves of Ritual Murder scares swept over Eastern Europe between 1928 and 1934. The Nazis, of course, pulled out all the stops and in 1934 Julius Streicher's *Der Sturmer* devoted a special twelve-page issue to the revival of all the old Ritual Murder accusations. Here at home the *American Jewish Yearbook* of 1929 reported the following incident: "On Saturday, September 22nd, 1928, a four year old girl, the daughter of one of the residents of Massena, in St. Lawrence County, New York, disappeared. On the following day, after a search for the child had proved vain, a State trooper interrogated one of the Jewish residents of the village and also the rabbi of the congregation as to whether the custom exists among the Jews to offer human sacrifice. The rabbi indignantly resented . . . and later the trooper stated that the Mayor had been consulted on the matter and that it was he who had suggested that the rabbi be called to police headquarters for questioning. Toward the close of the following afternoon, the child was found in the woods about a mile from her home, where she had been lost."

in 1144, so the story goes, the corpse of a young skinner's apprentice named William was discovered in a wooded area near Norwich, England. A rumor started that he had been done in by Jews who had crucified him after the synagogue service during Passover, in mockery of the Passion of Christ. The body was brought back to town, tearfully paraded through the streets and interred with solemn ceremony in the local cathedral, where it promptly began to work miracles. An outraged mob set out after the Jews of Norwich, who saved themselves by taking refuge in the town fortress until Christian tempers had cooled, although one of the leaders of the Jewish group was murdered shortly after by one of his debtors seeking a profitable revenge for the Lord.

Other cases followed in rapid succession: the Jews of Gloucester were accused of torturing and crucifying a Christian youth named Harold and dropping his mutilated corpse in the Severn River. Similar reports from Bury St. Edmunds and Bristol firmed up the popular conviction that the Jews were stepping up their campaign against the Savior through members of His flock. In all these affairs the corpse and assorted relics of the victims were enshrined and venerated in the traditions of the Christian martyr-saint.

In France meanwhile, the first instance of a Jewish Ritual Murder was being recorded in the town of Blois, where a Christian servant appeared before the town mayor with a horrifying announcement. He had been watering his master's horse in the nearby Loire River when this rich Jew, riding a fancy horse, appeared and threw a mysterious bundle into the river. The mayor, who was obviously more sophisticated in these matters than the servant, reported to his overlord, Count Theobald of Chartres, that the Jews of Blois had just crucified a Christian child in celebration of Passover. Count Theobald immediately had all the Jews in town thrown into prison pending further investigation. But further investigation by torture brought nothing to light. The rack could not jog memories of a recent crucifixion, no mother appeared looking for a lost child, no corpus delecti could be found, and the Christian servant was unable to identify the man who had thrown the "body" into the river. So the servant was subjected to the medieval lie-detecting device of the water test. He was set in the middle of the river in a boat filled with water. When the boat failed to sink, no doubt remained that he had been telling the truth and that the Jews were liars as well as murderers. Count Theobald therefore sentenced the "ringleaders" to burning at the stake. Thirty-four men and seventeen women perished in the flames, and the chronicler of these events recorded the deed for posterity in the dispassionate tone of the professional historian:

> *Theobald, Count of Chartres, caused several Jews of Blois to be burnt, because they had crucified a Christian child at the celebration of their Passover and had thrown its body into the Loire.*

The most celebrated of all the Jewish Ritual Murders of the Middle Ages was that of Little Hugh of Lincoln. In August of 1255 the body of a lad named Hugh, who had been missing for three weeks, was discovered in an open cesspool near the home of a singularly unfortunate Jew by the name of Copin. How Little Hugh got there nobody knew, although a plausible explanation is that like most little boys he wasn't looking where he was going and he fell in. To the thirteenth century mind, however, it was obvious that Little Hugh was the victim of a Jewish crucifixion. His body was reverently extricated from the cesspool and removed to the cathedral, convoyed by the local church dignitaries and town officials, amid much chanting and waving of crosses and candles, while the general populace wept. In the cathedral Little Hugh was laid to rest in a special shrine, with various relics scattered about him which began effecting stupendous cures among the ailing Christians of Lincoln.

Retribution followed swiftly. The Jew Copin, near whose home the body was found, "confessed" under torture that Little Hugh had played the part of Jesus in a recent Ritual Murder. King Henry (III) himself, on hearing the news, hustled over to Lincoln to look into the matter personally. In a preliminary demonstration of the royal justice, Copin was tied to a horse's tail, dragged up and down the city streets and then hanged. The other Jews implicated in the affair—almost one hundred—were then carried off to London where some were hanged and the others were left to ponder their sacrilege in prison. The case of Little Hugh—or "Saint Hugh" as the locals quickly dubbed him—soon entered into the body of English folklore. Chaucer speaks of him in the *Canterbury Tales* and he became a favorite topic of numerous ballads recited by traveling bards all over the Christian West.

By the thirteenth century so many accusations of Jewish Ritual Murder were being noised around Europe that Christians were easily persuaded to believe the worst on the flimsiest evidence. On one occasion, for example, a river ship from Cologne put into the Rhine town of Boppard. There the passengers saw the body of a Christian woman who had apparently just died. Somebody suddenly remembered that a ship loaded with Jews had recently passed that way and it was immediately agreed that the corpse on the pier had been left by these Jews after a Ritual Murder at sea. The Christians set sail after the Jewish ship, overtook and boarded it and hurled its passengers into the Rhine. In Mainz, on the strength of a whispered rumor that the Jews of that city had bought and crucified a Christian child a mob set fire to the synagogue and burned to death some two hundred Jews inside.

The same mentality which gave birth to the Jewish Ritual Murder began early to add some refinements to it. The Jews were supposed to have a particular fancy for their victim's heart. While he was still suspended from the Cross, they would cut a hole in his side, reach in and tear out the heart. Then they would grind it up with specially selected herbs into a portion of formidable but undefined proportions. The blood was also drained from the body and turned to a variety of practical uses: to add flavor to unleavened bread and body to the Seder wine and to cure disease. It was also the basic ingredient in loathsome witch-brews guar-

JEWS TAKING THE BLOOD FROM CHRISTIAN CHILDREN. (From the medieval *Book of the Cabala* of Abraham the Jew.)

anteed to proctect Jews from their enemies and to turn Christians into mad dogs.

Another favorite among these popular bedtime stories had the

Jews wreaking vengeance on a different Christ-substitute, the consecrated Communion wafer. The most common version told of Jews stabbing the wafer with sharp knives to make it spurt blood. Communion wafers, especially consecrated ones, were not items for public distribution, particularly to the sons of Moses. But Jewish cunning stopped at nothing. A Jew of Paris was burned alive on the charge of abusing a wafer which he had fished from the vomit of a sick woman just returned from Mass. A resourceful Jew of Brussels, who had apparently saved them up for years, was burned at the stake for mass murder because, it was said, he had stabbed sixteen such wafers until they dripped blood. A traffic in international wafer-smuggling was exposed by a Brussels Jewess who confessed to the illegal transportation of a case of stolen wafers to the Jews of Cologne for purposes of profanation. Advised of these doings, the authorities at Cologne rounded up the smugglers, who were hiding in the Jewish quarter, and burned them alive.

The ancient peoples of the Eastern Mediterranean believed that a slain god-substitute was certain to avenge himself on his murderers whenever the opportunity offered itself. The medieval man-in-the-street obviously thought so too. When the corpse of a martyred boy in Germany was tossed into the Rhine it not only insisted on floating but it radiated a continuous halo of light which finally led to its discovery and a proper punishment of the murderers. Another time, a drowned girl (crucifixion was for boys only) is said to have bled in the presence of the accused and to have raised her arms the second time they were brought into her presence. The most edifying example of heavenly revenge, however, occurred in Posen toward the end of the fourteenth century. A group of Jews participating in a wafer stabbing found to their dismay that the blood which spurted in their faces would not wash off. In desperation they sneaked out of town in the middle of the night and buried the wafer in a field. But the birds of the air kept circling over the fateful spot and the beasts of the field insisted on kneeling around it. The secret was thus discovered and the culprits, easily identified by their blood-stained faces, were bound together with dogs and burned to death, the terrified dogs tearing at the Jews' flesh as the flames crackled around them.

By the end of the fourteenth century the Jews in northern Europe had entered upon their darkest days since the time of Nebuchadnezzar. In the Spanish kingdoms south of the Pyrenees medieval Jewry for many years followed a different and happier course. The howling of the great masses for Jewish blood was yet to be heard there. When it was, the fate of Spain's Jews would one day be sealed in the name of her first Grand Inquisitor, Thomas de Torquemada.

CHAPTER 2

The Golden Age

PONTIUS PILATE, who authorized the execution of Jesus of Nazareth in Jerusalem, was an otherwise obscure governor of a small Roman province on the eastern fringe of a rapidly expanding empire. The Romans at that time were in the middle stages of their long campaign to confer the blessings of the Roman Peace upon the anicent world. The Jews were but one of many old civilizations uprooted by Roman ambition. By the time of Christ there were already the beginnings of an internationalized Judaism distinct from the homebound traditions of the Old Testament. Jewish traders and merchants began to appear in the far corners of the empire. Jewish administrators were encouraged to enter the civil service as minor functionaries in a growing imperial bureaucracy, and Jewish young men found adventurous careers in the Roman armies.

By the end of the first Christian century small pockets of transplanted Israelites were scattered throughout the West. To Spain (as elsewhere) they came as traders from Asia Minor and Egypt along the great sea routes followed by their Phoenician kinsmen many centuries before. There they were joined by veterans from the imperial legions, rewarded by a grateful and practical government with land grants on the sparsely populated frontier. Wherever they found themselves they settled down to start a new life, mingling with other elements of the local population in the everyday matters of economic and political life, while holding fast to the religious and social traditions of the old country.

Meanwhile, other Jews—heretics from the faith of their fathers—came preaching along the great highways to Rome. The young Galilean executed in Jerusalem, they said, was the Son of God, and was very much alive. His fellow Jews having rejected Him, His followers were come to offer to the Gentiles the chance for salvation which the Jews had spurned.

The Roman authorities took none of this very seriously. Their experience as conquerors had made them familiar with all kinds of amusing local superstitions, and their talent for administration had taught them the folly of interfering with harmless religious aberrations. Besides, this newest religion was nothing really new: the East abounded with mystery cults built around some savior who had died and risen again. So long as these self-styled Christians from the back country were willing to behave themselves, they could preach as they pleased.

It soon became apparent, however, that the Christians were an unusual breed of believers. To live and let live was a dereliction of duty for men exalted by the Truth. For a Christian there could be no compromise with public law or false gods where matters of salvation were concerned. Consequently, while the transplanted Jews were sharing in the general security and prosperity of the Roman world and practicing their religion in relative peace, their schismatic brethren were being immortalized for both eternity and posterity in the sacred history of the early Christian martyrs. Saint Paul (Saul the Jew) and Saint Peter (Simon the Jew) were among the first to go, probably on orders of Nero. The Roman historian, Tacitus, who lived during these times, disapproved of Nero's motives, but he shared the general sentiment toward the new sect.

The Emperor (he wrote) *punished with every refinement these*

THE GOLDEN AGE

notoriously depraved Christians, as they are called. Dressed in wild animals' skins, they were torn apart by dogs, or crucified, while yet others were turned into torches to be lit after dark as substitutes for daylight. Nero provided his gardens for the spectacle, and exhibited displays in the circus, at which he mingled with the crowd or stood in a chariot dressed as a charioteer. Despite their guilt as Christians, and the ruthless punishment they deserved, the victims were pitied. For it was felt that they were being sacrificed to one man's brutality rather than to the national interest.

It took three centuries more for Christianity to achieve any significant success in Rome. In 310 the worldly Emperor Constantine, for reasons still known only to himself and Jehovah, announced his conversion to the True Faith and made it clear that he expected all loyal men to do likewise. With imperial preference now reserved for Christians, the aristocratic pagans and agile courtiers of Constantine's retinue made what one cynic described as an ungodly rush for holy orders. Almost overnight the once despised and persecuted sect of slaves and social dregs became the all powerful and persecuting official religion of the vast Roman Empire. The resistance of false believers soon crumbled before the onslaught of Truth verified by the imperial sword.

The only noteworthy holdouts against the new spirit of universal brotherly love were the Jews, who remained stubbornly unconvinced of the unique qualifications of the Savior despite the proof offered by the Emperor's sudden conversion. Instead they clung perversely to the God of Moses and the teachings of their rabbis. By remaining as they were—islands of non-belief in the orthodox Western sea—they became a race apart, easily identifiable by their differences from their neighbors and readily available as legitimate objects of popular hatred and murder.

The spirit of martyrdom sometimes has a less savory counterpart in the spirit of persecution. The history of Christianity until relatively modern times provides some bloody examples of this double-edged passion. The heroic self-sacrifice of the despised

Christian minorities before Constantine was transformed into a zealous pogrom against non-believers with the conversion of that illustrious emperor. And the Jews, naturally, were destined to be a major target. Christianity was built on the ancient Jewish faith. The Jews, however, had refused to accept the radical innovations introduced by Jesus and Paul. It became their function, therefore, to prove the sanctity of such refinements by suffering the consequences of their own rejection of them. The centuries which followed the establishment of Christian orthodoxy in the West were marked by a constancy of anti-Semitic sentiment and intermittent periods of harassment and of persecution climaxed by the horrors described in the preceding chapter.

In Spain, meanwhile, Jewish life was taking a happier course. In the late sixth century, when Rome and her greatness were but fading memories, Mohammed the Prophet was acquainting his Arabian countrymen with the revelations of Allah. Within a few years after the Prophet's death, his Moorish followers began carving out a world empire which extended from Persia in the East, westward across North Africa to the Atlantic Ocean. In 711 the Moorish tide flooded across the Straits of Gibraltar and did not stop until it reached into the southern stretches of France.

The Spanish Jews welcomed the Moors as a relief from the periodic persecutions of their Christian neighbors. Under the rule of Islam a great cultural revival swept over the Peninsula. While the rest of medieval Europe was subduing the intellect to heavenly dogma, Arabian and Jewish scholars of Cordova and Toledo, Granada and Seville, made Spain the exclusive center of the arts and sciences and the unique home of civilization for the whole of the Western world. Every Spanish city had its prosperous Jewish quarter made up of free citizens subject to none of the economic, social or political restrictions which plagued their kinsmen in the rest of Europe. This was the "Renaissance," the "Golden Age" of Jewry in the European world, now universally admired by the historians of Judaism.

Even when the Moorish flood began to recede southward down

THE GOLDEN AGE 23

the Peninsula, the Jews continued to flourish under the rule of Christian monarchs in such newly established kingdoms as Aragon and Castile. Their numbers alone made them an important element of the population, perhaps as much as one fifth of a total of eight million by the late thirteenth century. They lived unmolested in their own communities, with their synagogues, their own law codes and courts, and their own rights of worship without interference. They were constantly sought after as administrators, tax-collectors and diplomats in the service of their Christian overlords. The high quality of their craftsmanship in the various trades made them the leaders in such industries as cloth, furniture, clothing and jewelry. They shared with the Moors the reputation of being the best physicians of the Middle Ages and were employed by the princes and kings of the land, who found the Jews' scientific knowledge more efficacious than the Christian methods of prayer and exorcism. In fact, the era of greatest Jewish prosperity—the "zenith of Spanish—Jewish culture," as Jewish historians call it—came in the twelfth and thirteenth centuries at the height of the Christian Reconquest against the Moors.

Modern historians—whether Jewish, Christian or neuter—describe with awe the power and influence which the Jews exercised over Spanish life in this period, as though that apparent domination were a reality independent of everything except the special cunning or superior talents of the Jews themselves. The suddenness of the disasters which subsequently fell upon the Jews seems almost to catch the historians by surprise and they seek to explain it as a spontaneous reversal of history brought about by popular indignation over the reality of Jewish domination. I must confess to a somewhat different view of this matter, namely, that Jewish power and influence was a delusion which the Jews themselves very likely shared, and that the merciless annihilations of the fourteenth and fifteenth centuries were the inevitable consequence of an anti-Semitic tradition born in the West with the conversion of Constantine.

Unless we assume that every one of the million or more Jews

of Spain was a combination of Svengali and Rasputin, we must define power in relation to freedom of action. The Jews, despite the seeming independence of their own communities, were the personal property of the Crown—the "King's Jews." The Jewish magistrate who ruled the ghetto was directly responsible to the royal authority. The latter could do as he pleased with his Jews: he could favor them, exalt or abase them, caress or kick them according to his fancy. The only rights they had were those which the monarch chose to recognize; the only privileges they enjoyed were those he chose to bestow; the only power they exercised was the authority he was willing to delegate to them in his own name and for just so long as it suited him.

For several centuries it suited the royal fancy very well to exploit the Jews liberated from Moorish dominion. As merchants and craftsmen they were an economic asset to the state. Accustomed over the centuries to the subtle negotiations necessary to their mere survival, they were astute advisers in matters of state. Their learning and scholarship gave lustre to the royal court and pleasing epithets to kingly patrons like Alfonso the Wise of Castile. Their brains and courage made them valuable allies as supply masters and soldiers in the continuing Crusade against the power of Islam which still held sway over great areas of Spain. But, most important of all, the Jews provided a seemingly inexhaustible supply of money— a great brood sow pumping out a never-ending flow of gold for her royal owners. They paid all kinds of taxes—special levies for special purposes, taxes for the privilege of being Jews, taxes for war, for peace, tithes for the Church of the True Faith, and confiscatory levies for behavior displeasing to the Crown. "The Jews," said Alfonso III of Aragon, "are the strongbox and treasury of kings." "Without the sons of Jacob," went the royal chant, "our finances would go to ruin."

The great literary epic of the Spanish Reconquest was (and is still) the *Poem of the Cid*. Written by an anonymous patriot around the middle of the twelfth century, it tells of the deeds of a half-mythical hero of bygone days who dedicated his life to the Crusade against the Moors. The opening scene shows us two Jews counting their ill-gotten gains in the hand-rubbing tradition of the universal Shylock. Enter the Cid—brave, bold, defender of virtue, pale death of the Saracen. Two chests full of treasure he brings to exchange for Jewish gold. The Jews drive a hard bargain. The Cid accepts. The Jews open the chests to find sand instead of treasure. But the brave Cid is already beyond the horizon exterminating the infidel.

The *Chronicle of the Cid*, which appeared about a century later, is an extended biography in prose of the popular Moor-slayer, and closes on an anti-Semitic note of miraculous proportions. After his death the Cid's body, in full battle dress and with sword at his side, was placed in an ivory chair and installed in the monastery at Cardena. On the seventh anniversary of his passing, while the abbot of the local monastery was preaching a memorial sermon to a great concourse in front of the cloister, a Jew sneaked into the sacred room to profane the hero by pulling his beard. But when he reached out his hand, the Cid pulled out his sword and the cowardly Jew screamed with fright and swooned at his feet. When he was finally revived, he was so overcome by this miracle that he begged for Christian baptism, which was speedily granted amid cries of joy from the assembled multitude. "And from that day forward," our chronicler reports, "he remained in the monastery as long as he lived, doing service to the body of the Cid."

Similar sentiments, elaborated in more prosaic detail, appear in the famous *Siete Partidas*, a lengthy compend of wisdom and nonsense published in the same golden era as the *Chronicle of the Cid* and sponsored by the most celebrated of all patrons of Jewish scholarship, King Alfonso the Wise of Castile. The Jews, wrote King Alfonso, live among Christians only on sufferance. They descend from the ancient tribe of Judah, noblest and bravest of all the tribes, the chosen people of God, honored and respected amongst all people. But when Christ came to confer new honors

RITUAL MURDER OF SIMON OF TRENT (ITALY). (From a 15th century woodcut.)

and privileges upon them, they rejected Him and dishonored Him by making Him die vilely on the Cross. Because of this wicked treachery, God deprived them of their ancient honors and privileges and decreed that ever since that evil day they should always be ruled by others. Never again would they enjoy the honor of high office from which to rule over the followers of Him whom they had crucified. They would live forever in captivity, a constant reminder to all men that they descended from the once proud race which crucified our Lord Jesus Christ. And, the wise Alfonso noted, even now they seek to repeat the abomination of Calvary by the ritual murder of Christian children:

> *We have heard that, in some places, the Jews, on Good Friday, have commemorated and do commemorate the Passion of our Lord Jesus Christ in a mocking manner by stealing Christian children and placing them on the Cross, or by making waxen images and crucifying them when they cannot obtain Christian children. Therefore we order that if henceforth there is any report that such a thing has been done anywhere within our domains, if it can be ascertained, that all persons implicated in such a deed be seized and brought before the king, and after he determines the truth, they shall be executed in the most vile manner, whoever they may be.*

In keeping with his thesis of a perpetual Babylonian Captivity, Alfonso materializes the Divine Will in the form of repressive legislation. Jews must wear a special badge for easy identification. Jews and Christians are forbidden to eat or bathe together under penalty of fine and imprisonment, or to sleep together under penalty of death. Any Jew who becomes a Christian shall enjoy all the civil as well as spiritual blessings of that happy estate. If one spouse accepts Christianity, he (or she) may leave the unregenerated partner and marry anyone else with no legal complications. Any Jew who tries to prevent his well-intentioned kinsman from becoming a Christian, or who would seduce a true believer into the errors of Judaism, shall be burned alive. A Christian who succumbs to such blandishments shall likewise be burned alive. No Jew may say anything critical of the Christian Faith, since Christianity is the Truth and Judaism is a lie. If a consecrated Communion wafer should be carried through the streets in a religious parade or en route to the bedside of an immobilized believer, the Jew must show proper respect to the reincarnated Body of the Lord which his ancestors so disgracefully dishonored. He should kneel down when it passes by or else get off the street. Failure to do one or the other would land him in jail, assuming that he survived the indignation of the devout.

The deputies to the regional councils (*Cortes*) of the new Spanish kingdoms needed no urging to follow the royal lead. The numerous Cortes of the thirteenth and fourteenth centuries ground out a comprehensive body of legislation designed to harass the Jews at every turn. They were forbidden to serve as physicians to Christians, to take Christian names, wear rich clothing or furs, or to use fancy saddles for their horses. No Jew could give evidence in court against a Christian and no Jewish judge could preside over a case involving a Jew and a Christian. All material offensive to Christians must be removed from Jewish prayerbooks. No Jew could live in a Christian home except as a slave and no Jewish baby could be suckled by a Christian wetnurse.

The Spanish Church, brandishing the spiritual sword of excommunication, soon joined the hunt. An ecclesiastical council at Zamora in 1313 denounced the Jews as serpents in the Christian Eden and issued a battery of edicts ordering an end to all social intercourse between the races. Subsequent councils directed the Faithful to drive away Jews loitering near Christian churches, forbade them to attend Jewish weddings and funerals or to act as godparents to Jewish children, or to employ a Jewish physician, since it was well known that the latter employed their medical skill to murder their Christian patients.

These and similar restrictions, although indifferently enforced, were nevertheless a constant reminder to the Jews of the capricious nature of their existence. The sons of Moses, however, had long ago learned to live with uncertainty as the price of being different. If the Spanish Jews did have any comforting delusions about their relative immunity from any ultimate disaster they must surely have been dispelled by the civil war which broke out in Castile in 1350. Peter the Cruel, who became king in that year, lived down his nickname in his attitude toward the Jews, treating them with special favor. Henry of Trastamara, bastard brother to Peter, launched a rebellion to take the throne for himself. The conflict raged across Castile for almost twenty years, with Henry winning popular support by legalizing his rebellion in the name of a crusade against that "Jew son of a bitch" Peter and the Jew conspirators who were supporting him.

As testimony to the virtues of their leader, Henry's armies sacked the ghetto of Toledo and slaughtered some twelve hundred of its inmates without regard to sex or age. In 1360, when he seized the city of Najara, Henry further sanctified his Cause by ordering the massacre of all the Jews in town, and at irregular but calculated intervals during the next ten years, similar instances of political trimming resulted in the indiscriminate murder of thousands of Jews all over Castile. In 1369, the assassination of the "Jew King" Peter seated his rebel brother on the throne of Castile.[1] Henry of Trastamara, who was never really mad at the Jews anyway, assumed the burdens of royal responsibility with the assistance of the Jewish talent he employed for the administration of his kingdom.

Any government which singles out a special group as a legitimate object of hatred and violence is playing a dangerous game. The great masses of the People, encouraged by the example of their betters, are likely to take matters into their own hands. And unless their enthusiasm can be limited to immediate practicable ends, the government runs the double risk of seeing its own authority undermined and of being forced to placate the People by adopting extreme measures hurtful to its own practical interests. The Spanish monarchs were alert to such unpleasant possibilities and they vigorously discouraged unauthorized violence against Jews. By the fourteenth century, however, such acts were becoming more and more frequent. In the northern kingdom of Navarre the exhortations of a Franciscan friar named Pedro Olli-

---

[1] "Oh noble Pedro, glory once of Spain,
Whom Fortune held so high in majesty,
Well ought men read thy piteous death with pain!
Out of thy land thy brother made thee flee;
And later, at a siege, by scheme crafty,
Thou wert betrayed, and led into his tent,
Where he then, and with his own hand, slew thee,
Succeeding to thy realm and government."
—Chaucer, *Canterbury Tales*

goyen in 1328 stirred up a wholesale slaughter of at least six thousand Jews. Twenty years later the Black Death hysteria slopped over the Pyrenees from northern Europe and brought on more killing which was stopped only by the determined action of the royal authorities. The next forty years were punctuated by growing numbers of popular attacks on Jewish ghettos throughout the land. The ferocity with which these assaults were punished suggests a growing sense of royal desperation in the face of a populace ready to explode in mass murder. The People of Spain were about to take up the sword. The cruel year of 1391 was just ahead.

CHAPTER 3

1391

THE GREAT FIRES WHICH BURNED OUT the Jewish ghettos of Spain in 1391 were lit from the mouth of Archdeacon Ferdinand Martinez, canon of the cathedral of Seville. A man "more saintly than learned," one of his admirers once described him, on the widely held premise that these two qualities are mutually exclusive. He is, all the same, a type that History has always had to reckon with. Whether he be the Lord's Jew-Roaster in Germany, a prophet from the dungheaps of France, or a Spanish archdeacon in clerical weeds, he everywhere exhibits the stigmata of the inspired nihilist: virtue undefiled by honor, piety triggered by hate, and a sense of conviction which equates tolerance with treason—all fused into holy madness by a passion for violence and murder.

Martinez the Archdeacon had a single mission in life—to wipe out the Jews. With a mighty eloquence he preached the gospel of slaughter to excited mobs in the streets and churches of Seville. The Jews, he said, were infidel dogs, and their synagogues were houses of the Devil where three times each day they cursed Christ and all His sheep. It was therefore the sacred duty of Christians to kill the wicked sons of Moses. This was not Martinez the man speaking; these were the words of the ancient Prophets and of

Christ Himself, transmitted through their agent in Seville. He was accordingly in a position to guarantee absolution from all sin and the eternal bliss of Paradise to Jew-killers. And, with a sharp eye for terrestrial concerns, he promised his hearers that the royal authority would likewise concur in the heavenly scheme.

Whatever the Host of Heaven thought about the archdeacon's claims, their secular representatives—the kings of Castile—had some definite reservations. As we have seen, Henry of Trastamara had a taste for killing Jews himself: during his successful war against his brother Peter the Cruel he had massacred them by the thousands. However, his actions in that affair had stemmed from a calculated policy of statecraft. It was all right for the king to abuse the Jews—they were his property to do with as he pleased. But he was not going to allow his subjects to take the law into their own hands.

Henry's son, John I, shared his father's view. He too gratified his needs by an occasional persecution, but that was his royal right. The zeal of Archdeacon Martinez, he said, is "saintly and good," for the Jews indeed are a "wicked and perverse" people. Nevertheless, he insisted, they are "part of our treasure" and "under my protection and authority," and any necessary punishments will be administered "according to the law."

For years the roads from Seville to the royal court were traveled by couriers bearing petitions from the Jews begging for royal protection against the "lies and slanders" of the archdeacon. The Crown, in turn, sent repeated warnings to Martinez to stop agitating the populace to violence and sedition. To the complaints of the Jews Martinez replied with volleys of invective, asserting that if he had his way he would personally kill them all and level their synagogues to the ground. He also refused to concede that the king had any authority to interfere with the inalienable right of Christians to kill Jews or with the holy mission of the Lord's personal representative on earth—Martinez, that is.

In 1389 Martinez suddenly found himself facing a really formidable threat to his power. He had announced, in a recent sermon, that not even the Pope had the authority to allow Jews to build synagogues and live among Christians. For fourteen years the ecclesiastical shepherds had been standing silently by while the archdeacon vomited his hate on the Jews. But now he had ventured to question the authority of the Pope; now he was preaching not just mass murder, but heresy. His superior, the archbishop of Seville, immediately convoked a solemn council of learned theologians who summoned Martinez to appear before them and explain himself. By this time Martinez was beyond all authority except that from God above and the People below, and he told the council he would allow his opinions to be judged only by the good folk of Seville. Furious, the archbishop and council declared him to be a "contumacious rebel, obstinate in his error, and suspect of heresy," and ordered him to stop preaching, under pain of excommunication.

What happened next almost persuades us that Martinez did have a supernatural ally in the wings. The archbishop of Seville died within a few months and until his replacement could be sent in, Martinez was first in command. At almost the same time, King John I fell off his horse in a freak accident and was killed. He left a sickly son of tender years to succeed him and a conflict immediately broke out between opposing factions at the court over who was to run the government until the boy grew up. The result was political chaos, bringing a temporary halt to effective government in Castile.

Archdeacon Martinez would certainly have gone on with his work in any case. Mere human objections were nothing to a man whose head buzzed with heavenly voices. However, the fortuitous deaths of both the king and the archbishop suddenly opened the way to the ghetto of Seville. On March 15, 1391, Martinez celebrated Ash Wednesday with a thunderous sermon in the public square. The People, assembled in great numbers, howled and applauded. When they were well heated up, their Leader sent them out to scour the streets. Running in packs they began beating up Jews and robbing them. Those who escaped ran to the ghetto and locked themselves in. At any moment it seemed the whole city would be turned upside down. The governor and a body of magistrates, hoping to stop the disturbance short of revolution, seized two of the ringleaders and had them publicly flogged. This only enraged the mob even more and considerable bloodshed and plunder followed before the authorities were able to restore some semblance of order.

Three months later the final storm broke. At the first flush of dawn on June 6, 1391, by an obviously prearranged plan, the People of Seville suddenly burst from their houses, joined ranks all over town and converged on the ghetto. In their first onslaught they smashed down the gates and stormed over the walls. All day they raped, murdered, looted and burned. Men, women and children were axed, hammered, bludgeoned and chopped to death, while the hot voice of Archdeacon Martinez kept urging his army on to even greater slaughter in the name of the Lord. In one single day four thousand Jews were murdered. More thousands averted death by shouting out their desire for Christian baptism. Others fled into the country to become wanderers in a hostile land. A miserable remnant somehow survived and slowly gathered itself together after the horror had passed. The ghetto became a Christian prize. The houses and shops were taken over by the Faithful and the synagogues were purified with holy water and transformed into Christian churches. A whole Jewish community of thirty thousand souls, rich in the accumulated traditions of centuries, had disappeared in one day.

Even stranger than the convulsive suddenness of the disaster of Seville was the incredible speed with which similar massacres broke out all over Spain. During the next three months the spirit of Ferdinand Martinez erupted in violence and murder in at least seventy cities. In the north the bloody tide spilled across the Pyrenees into France; in the east it ran red into the Mediterranean Sea; in the south and west it did not stop until it reached the frontiers of Moorish Granada and Portugal. At Cordova, the birthplace of Moses Maimonides, greatest Jewish philosopher of the medieval world, the ancient Jewish quarter was reduced to ashes and two thousand corpses were left rotting in the streets. A like fate struck Toledo, center of European learning in the West, where Jewish savants kept alive the forgotten wisdom of the ancients. There the largest Jewish community in Spain was destroyed August 5, on the Fast Day when the Jews were mourning the destruction of Jerusalem by Babylonian armies two thousand years before.

Holy days, particularly Christian ones, were a popular choice for massacres. The first outbreak in Seville occurred on Ash Wednesday. The Toledo massacre fell on a Jewish Fast Day which was also the Christian Feast of Saint Dominic. The Feast of Saint Lorenzo was celebrated by wholesale atrocities in Perpignan and Gerona on opposite sides of the Pyrenees. One of the most spectacular of all Feast Day celebrations took place in Valencia in honor of Saint Christopher, barely a month after the purging of Seville. Refugees from the archdeacon's crusade began arriving at the port of Valencia with tales of horror and violence in other places. The appearance of these wretched wanderers stimulated the normally sluggish pulses of the local riffraff, who began stoning Jewish men and growling lewd songs to the women. Within a few days the Jews had locked themselves inside their houses and the city fathers had posted heavy guards to patrol the ghetto day and night.

Children, as every child soon discovers, make a game of everything, including persecution. The following Sunday morning a band of forty or fifty Valencian moppets, intoxicated by the assurance of their elders' approval, gathered in the public square for a little sport with the Jews. Waving small wooden Crosses and a large blue banner emblazoned with a white Crucifix, they marched on the Jewish quarter, a chorus of boy sopranos singing praises to the Savior and insults to His murderers. Other kids rushed to join the fun and by the time they arrived at the ghetto they made a considerable little army. They milled around outside the entrance, hurling jeers and catcalls at the Jews inside, warning them that Archdeacon Martinez himself was on his way to Valencia to clean up the city. This was the Jews' last chance—they could take their choice between baptism and death.

The Jews quickly shut the gate into the ghetto, but not before a few of the boy soldiers in the front ranks were pushed inside by their comrades in back. One of the boys let out a bloodcurdling howl when the gate slammed shut on this hand. His companions on the outside went wild; they raced through the streets shouting that the Jews were killing Christian boys in the ghetto. The whole town came running, their numbers (and courage) reinforced by a detachment of soldiers who had been hanging around town looking for excitement while waiting to be shipped overseas to Italy. The mob began battering at the gates, which the Jews had hurriedly braced with heavy beams and chains. The town officials, whose frightened efforts to restore order almost got them killed as Jew-loving spoilsports, scurried off to the palace of the bishop of Valencia. There they begged their royal visitor, Don Martin of Aragon, brother of the king, to save the city from revolution. His Excellency mounted his horse, gathered his retinue about him, and set out for the ghetto. At the sight of the royal colors the besiegers grudgingly laid down their battering rams and opened a path for their duke. The latter called upon the Jews to open the gate so the People could see that their young Christian soldiers were unharmed. In return he promised to station his personal guard inside the ghetto to guarantee its safety.

Paralyzed by fear, the Jews either would not or could not open the barrier, and the royal effort to thwart the People's pleasures was dissipated in a renewed thrust at the gate, which suddenly gave way under the sheer weight of numbers. In this first assault one of the attackers was killed. A terrible silence—the aura of doom—fell over the crowd while the body was reverently passed through the mob and laid at the feet of the duke.

For one brief moment the world seemed to stand still, and the smell of Death hung heavy in the air. Then a roar from ten thousand throats split the skies, heralding the return of mankind to the kingdom of the jungle. A boiling mass of humanity poured into the ghetto through the gate, over the walls from the windows of adjoining houses. In blind terror the Jews locked themselves up in their homes, which quickly became their funeral pyres. Others ran into the synagogue seeking refuge in the otherworldly wisdom of their rabbis and elders. A pitifully small number, hoping to repeat the miracles of Gideon, armed themselves with crossbows and fought hopelessly until they were overwhelmed and slaughtered where they stood. The attacking horde set fire to the houses, beat down the doors of the warehouses and shops, looting them of property and women and killing the men and children. What they could not carry with them they smashed to rubble. Witnesses to these scenes reported that no sooner had one group abandoned a building they had just sacked when another band moved in behind them and stripped it right down to the nails in the walls.

> *In a short time* (we are told) *the entire ghetto was assaulted and looted and hundreds of bodies of both sexes and all ages lay strewn about in the streets and houses. Those Jews who escaped the killing ran, carrying cane crosses in their hands, to the churches, crying for baptism. The synagogues were purified and converted into churches. The ghetto of Valencia had disappeared. Its unfortunate inhabitants were scattered throughout the land, some in hiding, many others pretending a conversion which had been forced upon them, and all of them weeping over the loss of their worldly goods, their friends and their families.*

From the political point of view, which automatically excludes any moral considerations, the most disturbing aspect of the Massacres of 1391 was the complete breakdown of public order. In Seville and Valencia the local authorities were generally ignored. In other places they were not so lucky. The governor of Palma had his horse shot out from under him and was himself wounded while trying to quell the disorders there. The mob at Lerida stampeded right over the local magistrates and set fire to the town fortress, burning to death all the Jews inside along with the mayor who tried to protect them.

It was in Barcelona, where a Jewish community of ten thousand people disappeared via the twin roads of baptism and murder that the Great Massacre took on the dimensions of a proletarian revolution. On the Feast Day of Saint Dominic, a crowd of peasants, workers and screaming women, together with a group of sailors returning from the crusade at Valencia, set fire to the ghetto. Through the whole day and all during the night they murdered and plundered. The fleeing Jews took refuge in the great castle fortress in the center of town and the local governor posted a heavy cordon of troops around it to discourage the "little people" from further attacks. The following morning—Sunday—he threw some forty of the ringleaders in jail and on Monday he sentenced them to hang as an example to the rest. But when the martyrs were brought out for execution their homespun disciples, to the chant of "Long live the People," hurled themselves on the governor and his colleagues, killing one of them and trampling the rest under foot. They broke into the jail and freed all the prisoners. Then they chopped down the city gates while others climbed up to the bell towers of the churches and rang the bells to summon the peasants from the fields to join the revolution. All through the night on Monday the "little people" swirled around the city brandishing torches and shouting dark vengeance on the "big people" who were trying to oppress them.

On Tuesday they stormed the city hall and ransacked it, building great bonfires of the public documents and town records. Then they threw themselves at the castle fortress, demanding death or baptism for the Jews inside. The defenders, including the Jews themselves, fought back desperately and the battle raged until the next day before the castle fell. Some of the Jews killed themselves with their own hands; others flung themselves from the walls. The remainder were called upon to accept immediate baptism. Those who refused were killed on the spot and their corpses dragged about the city streets; the rest were hustled off to the baptismal font and purified. The Jews who had somehow escaped were rooted out of their hiding places and destroyed without mercy.

By the end of the summer of 1391 many of the Jewish communities of Spain, for centuries the repositories of learning, culture and industry for the whole Peninsula, had entirely disappeared. Some of them never recovered. Others were painfully rebuilt to provide future sport for the next generation of destroyers until their final extinction under the relentless holiness of Torquemada. The spoils were divided among the Christian victors: synagogues were converted into churches, the Faithful moved into former Jewish homes and took over their shops and warehouses. In Ciudad Real even the Jewish cemetery was the object of an untidy legal squabble among the Crown, nobility and Church. The latter finally secured possession and the Dominican order apparently sanctified the old graveyard with a new monastery, setting a pious example for Torquemada to follow in Avila a century later.

The number of Jews killed in the Massacres of 1391 is usually estimated at fifty thousand. Nobody will ever really know how many perished, however, for it is only in modern times, with its enthusiasm for bookkeeping, that Westerners have begun to keep records of the Jews they murder. Nor can we do more than guess at the number of refugees, although we do know that many of the North African towns along the Barbary Coast were flooded with Jews seeking peace under the rule of the Moslems.

By far the greatest number accepted baptism in preference to death. An official report made five days after the massacre at Valencia announces that the Jews there begged for baptism in such large numbers that the supply of holy oil would long since have diminished had it not been replenished by a happy succession of miracles. In some towns the Jews forestalled a massacre by asking for baptism at the first sign of trouble. The total of such conversions throughout Spain in the spring and summer of 1391 varies from half a million to over two million, depending on whose guess the reader prefers. And once a Jew had committed himself to Christianity, no matter the circumstances, there was no turning back. In Teruel, for example, a young woman "convert" was heard to say in public that she still felt a yearning for the faith of Moses. The next morning she was found in a ditch at the edge of town with a knife through her heart. The conclusion of local criminologists was that she had done herself in "at the suggestion of the Devil," which the townfolk accepted as a perfectly reasonable solution to the whole affair.

Saint Vincent Ferrer

Not so many years ago (writes a contemporary of Torquemada) *there was a man, native of the city of Valencia, named friar Vincent Ferrer, of the order of Preachers. He was a very famous theologian and wondrous preacher, a person of very pure life and saintly habits. In his lifetime he never ceased to illuminate the divine cult and exalt the Holy Faith. In public he preached and taught, exhorting, admonishing, advising and persuading, not only with fitting words and holy doctrine but by wondrous examples and habits and lessons. And as a result of the miracles which God performed because of this man's merits, Pope Calixtus III canonized him and recorded his name among the Blessed. For God, who rewards the good, performed miracles through his works during his life and after his death. So it was that, being of such a holy life and great eloquence, and imbued with such saintly doctrine, he pointed out to the Jews, by strong arguments and evident reason, all the errors and manifest deceptions by which they were blinding themselves. And in this manner he converted many of them to the holy faith. Having learned from him that the Christian religion, our faith, was both holy and true, they were baptised of their own free will and received all the sacraments of the Church.*

Perhaps. There are, however, more prosaic accounts of friar Vincent's work by those who knew him when he was a mere man. From these we learn that he first came into public prominence during the Massacre of 1391 in his native city of Valencia. He appeared suddenly at the height of the slaughter, calling upon the Jews to accept the saving waters of Christian baptism. Inspired by the vast number of conversions he made that day, he thenceforth dedicated his life to missionary work among the Jews. For the next twenty years he traveled the length and breadth of the Spanish Peninsula, winning souls to Christ. His eloquence, it is reported, was stupendous. Although his speech was Catalan, his words were clearly understood by Greeks, Moors, Frenchmen, Italians, Hungarians and Germans. So great were his powers that his mere presence was enough to heal the sick and restore the dead to life.

Friar Vincent was fired by apocalyptic visions. Convinced that the end of the world was at hand, he knew that mankind could be saved only by adopting the True Faith. Through the land he marched, escorted by a company of flagellants and spearmen, a Crucifix in one hand and the Torah in the other, calling on the Jews to accept the Redeemer and save their souls from perdition. Where he went, holiness stalked the streets, purifying the world for the coming Day of Judgment. From a special platform in the center of town he recited with sobs the sufferings of Jesus and the horrors of permitting Jews to mingle freely with Christians, calling on Heaven and the king to separate from the Faithful all Jews who refused to see the Truth. By night his company of disciples marched through the streets in great torchlight parades flogging themselves with knotted cords, singing psalms and summoning repentant sinners to salvation.

In most cases these pyrotechnics were enough to bring results, for the Jews had already been coaxed by the Massacres of 1391 into a willingness to accept baptism. But when they still proved to be obstinate, friar Vincent could show his claws. Raising his Crucifix on high, and backed by the excited mob, he would thrust his way into the synagogues, drive the money changers from their temple and consecrate it in the name of the Blessed Virgin as a Christian church.

Meanwhile, the Crown of Castile, in response to the People's voice and its own inclinations, was contemplating new and more extensive legal restrictions on the Jews who still persisted in clinging to their ancestral faith. Action was temporarily delayed by the death in 1406 of Henry (III) the Invalid. His son and successor, John II, was only two years old, so once again the government reverted to a regency, this time in the persons of the Queen-mother Catalina and her brother-in-law Don Ferdinand of Antequera.

Despite the exhortations of friar Vincent and his like-minded colleagues at court, the regents of Castile were exasperatingly slow to take action against the Jews. But then that sure stimulus to action—the Ritual Murder charge—was brought into play to help achieve the desired end. By a truly remarkable coincidence, during a visit of Queen-mother Catalina to Segovia in 1410, a group of local Jews were accused of attempting abominations on a consecrated Communion wafer. After stabbing it for a while they threw it into a cauldron of boiling water. To their horrified amazement the wafer kept popping out of the water and remaining suspended in the air. Some of the Jews were so impressed by this miracle that they were converted on the spot and ran with the wafer to the nearby Dominican monastery where they blurted out the whole story.

The news was immediately conveyed to the Queen-mother, who ordered a vigorous investigation. Among those implicated was Don Meyer Alguades, the royal physician. Under protracted torture he not only confessed to participating in the wafer plot but also to poisoning the late king (Henry III). He and his accomplices were dragged through the streets of Segovia, then hanged, then pulled apart, and their synagogue was turned into the Church of Corpus Christi as grim reciprocity for their sacrilege on the Body of our Lord.

Friar Vincent was immediately called to the court for consultation, where he urged the Queen-mother to take the strongest possible measures against those Jews whose blind obstinacy still shut out the Light of the Evangel. On January 2, 1412, Queen Catalina issued the celebrated Ordinances of 1412. His work at court completed, friar Vincent took his departure for other parts where there still remained much work to be done.

Where Martinez of Seville had sown, Vincent of Valencia had reaped a fat harvest. The Ordinances of 1412 were the second act of a deadly drama which opened at Seville in 1391. (The final act only awaited the coming of Thomas de Torquemada.) The Jews were now all confined to ghettos, which were to be completely walled in and provided with only one gate. They were forbidden to leave the country or even to change their residence from one town to another. Contact with Christians was likewise taboo: they could not transact business with them nor hire Christians as servants or as nurses for their children, nor eat, drink or bathe with Christians, nor work in Christian houses or on Christian lands, nor attend feasts, weddings or funerals with them. Christians were not allowed to enter the ghetto, and both Christians and Jews were forbidden to visit each other in sickness, exchange gifts, or engage one another in conversation.

Jews were further barred from public office, service as tax-collectors, and the practice of medicine and surgery. In fact, all but the most menial employments were denied to them: they could no longer work as grocers, apothecaries, farriers, blacksmiths, peddlers, carpenters, tailors, barbers or butchers. To make identification easy and contamination difficult, rigid rules of dress and toilet were laid down. Jews were required to put aside all jewelry and refinements of dress in favor of a standardized long cloak of the coarsest materials, decorated only by a red Jew badge which they must wear at all times. Both men and women were forbidden to cut their hair, and the men were also prohibited from trimming their beards.

The degradation of the Jews was virtually complete, and one Solomon Alami, an unhappy victim of the People's voice, wrote:

They forced strange clothing on us. They kept us from trade, farming and the crafts. They forced us to grow our beards and our hair long. Inmates of palaces were driven into wretched hovels and dark low huts. Instead of the rustle of silk, we were forced to wear miserable clothes, which drew scorn and contempt upon us. The rich tax-farmers sank into poverty, for they knew no trade by which to make a living. The artisans found no work because their trades were closed to them. Starvation stared everyone in the face, and children died on their mothers' knees from exposure and starvation.

The mass murders of 1391, the militant evangelism of Vincent Ferrer, and the uncompromising Ordinances of 1412, had erected a permanent wall of death and persecution around the Jews of Spain. Their only escape was through the doors of the Holy Church. A vast number chose baptism as the way out. As the number of Jews dwindled, a new class arose, like Phoenix, from the ashes of the ghetto. The *Marrano*, the *Anusim*, the *Converso* became a unique phenomenon in the historical landscape of the Spanish Peninsula.

CHAPTER 4

The Converso

IN THE WILD ENTHUSIASMS OF 1391 neither Christian nor Jew could be expected to consider, much less foresee the long range consequences of mass conversion at the point of the sword. The Christian saw only the final solution of an intolerable problem. The Jew saw only final and hopeless disaster. Yet a whole century was to pass before either result would be achieved.

As Jews, the children of Israel were being ground down in a new Egypt. As Christians they had the same rights and privileges as all other Christians, and a status higher than anything they had enjoyed even in the palmiest days of their Golden Age. They could live where they pleased, dress however they liked and enter whatever trade suited their fancy. No office—public, private or ecclesiastical— was closed to them.

The New Christian, or *Converso* as he was called,[1] prospered as never before, both in the trades and professions of his ancestors and in areas previously denied him as a Jew. He took his place in the law, administration, army and judiciary. He sat in municipal councils and dispensed wisdom in the universities—all places

---

[1] *Converso* literally means *convert,* but from the beginning it was applied to any Christian of Jewish ancestry, no matter how remote. The same is true of the terms *New Christian* and *Marrano* (swine), a very popular label as we might expect.

where the sons of Judah had never been seen before. Converso names dominated the rolls of jurists, historians, poets, scholars and men of letters. They appear as physicians, personal advisers, ambassadors and tutors of the blood of the realm. By the early fifteenth century we find Conversos exercising the offices of vice-chancellor, comptroller-general and royal treasurer of Aragon, while others of their tribe are presiding over both the supreme court of justice and the national Cortes. The admiral of Castile was a Converso, as was the chancellor of that kingdom, and their New Christian kin sat on the royal council.

If crossbreeding is the solution to the problem of "racial incompatibility," then it must be noted that the Converso made strenuous efforts to homogenize the races. Marriage between Jews and Christians had first been forbidden in Spain ten years after the conversion of Constantine. Sexual intercourse on an ad hoc basis was punished by death if the delinquents in the case were a male Jew and a lady Christian. The reverse arrangement, however, was widely tolerated in accordance with a self-indulgent tradition that is supposed to have some connection with prerogative and manliness among the males of the superior "race."

Under the new arrangement of Christian togetherness, however, the Converso had free access to the Christian marriage bed. Wealthy Conversos began buying either their own way or their children's way into aristocracy by marriage with the Old Christian nobility. Many of the latter, whose pride varied inversely with their income, found nothing dishonorable in this arrangement since the money they received had been purified at the baptismal font. The result was a massive transfusion of Jewish blood into virtually all the noble houses of Spain. In later years, when it was decided that a Jew was a Jew even when he was a Christian, there was a widespread demand for genealogists to trim the family tree, and historians broke out into controversies over family origins which are still going on today. In the fifteenth century, however, nobody realized the trouble they were causing for future generations.

Among the noble Conversos of the fifteenth century was Luis de Santangel, secretary to the royal household, who persuaded Ferdinand and Isabella to finance the dreams of Columbus. Don Juan Pacheco, marquis of Villena, was a virtual king-maker who aspired to the hand of Isabella of Castile only to lose out to another Converso, Ferdinand of Aragon.[1] Other families, such as the Caballerias, the Santa Fes and the Santa Marias, specialized in bishops and archbishops, physicians and theologians, and dedicated anti-Semites.

The influx of Conversos into the Church of the True Faith reached almost fantastic proportions. Beside the army of Conversos who served the banner of Christ as humble recruits in the priesthood and monastery, there were many others in the higher echelons. A random sample includes the following: royal chaplain to Henry III; confessor to Henry IV; two confessors to Queen Isabella; physician to the pope; papal nuncio to the court of Castile; general of the Geronomite order; grand masters of the orders of Santiago and Calatrava; bishops of Coria, Cordova, Cartagena, Burgos and Siguenza; archbishops of Granada and Toledo. Perhaps the most eminent of all the Conversos of this era were the cardinal of Saint Sixtus, Juan de Torquemada, and his celebrated nephew Thomas de Torquemada, future Inquisitor General of Spain.[2]

---

[1] Ferdinand's mother was Juana Enriquez of the Converso family of that name. At least it was widely believed in Ferdinand's day that the Enriquez family had a strain of Jewish blood. Some historians, as recently as 1954, have denied this, although their denials are based as much on indignation as on facts. On the other hand, the supporters of the "Jewish" thesis have no real facts to offer either. I have not taken any votes on the issue, but the more common view seems to be that Ferdinand was a Converso, although a sufficiently diluted one to satisfy (and vex) Jews and Christians alike. The greater number of opinions on one side probably proves nothing in itself except that more people prefer one theory than another. Genealogy is a difficult art under the best of conditions. When it is further complicated by the mystique of blood purity, it becomes a bottomless pit.

[2] The same general observations about King Ferdinand (above) apply to the Torquemadas. The stories that the scourge of Judaism himself had Jewish forebears were repeated five centuries later about the sadists around Adolf Hitler and even about *Der Fuehrer* himself. Historians of all persuasions, when they approach this

In the midst of his new freedom and prosperity the Converso often suffered from agonies of despair and guilt for having given up the faith of his ancestors. From the Inquisition trials of the late fifteenth century we get occasional glimpses of the agitated state of mind of some of the New Christians who simply could not adjust themselves to the circumstances forced upon them, despite the material advantages they provided. The conditions under which Inquisition trials were conducted make most testimony suspect. Since the present study is not designed to be a historical novel, therefore, I must resist the temptation to record the many juicy aberrations which crop up in these grim documents and limit myself to evidence which is both well substantiated and plausible.

In the privacy (and relative safety) of their homes some Conversos begged Jehovah for the deliverance He had granted in the past: "Oh God, deliver us as Thou delivered the people of Israel." "Oh God, deliver us from these oppressors who spy upon us and force us to betray the faith of our fathers." "Oh God, let the Turk come among us as thy avenging arm. Let him destroy the church of our oppressors and slay their holy men who make us live in deception among them."

Others sought refuge abroad. They sold all their worldly goods as quietly as possible so as not to excite the suspicion of their neighbors. With their families they made their way to the great port cities like Valencia and Barcelona where they sailed away to rejoin the ancestral faith in the ghettos of North Africa and the East. Many were apprehended on the docks and dragged out the rest of their miserable lives in the Spanish galleys. Still others suddenly dropped out of sight to reappear in the ghetto of a

---

question, stagger a little. Some appear to be undecided about which view they prefer to take because of the disturbing implications of either view, whatever "school" the investigator belongs to. A few resolve the dilemma by ignoring the subject entirely. As for myself, I have no preferences in the matter. Whether or not Torquemada was a full-Jew, half-Jew, fractional Jew, or pure Nordic, has no bearing on the events of his time. The most it can do is provide an interesting conversation piece for amateur psychologists and students of the bizarre.

strange city where, at the cost of their freedom and privileges as Christians and at the risk of being burned alive, they sought membership in the despised and persecuted minority of Jews.

The most pathetic were the great majority who, like most of us, are too frightened to do anything more than torture ourselves for our own fears. "Before the True Messiah can come," said one, "we Conversos will have to make retribution for having betrayed our faith." Every time he recited the mass, a Converso priest confessed, he froze with terror. When he raised the Host and repeated the words of Christ, "This is my Body," he expected at any moment to see the wrath of Jehovah come to melt him down into nothing. "I am neither a Jew, nor a Moor, nor a Christian," lamented another. "I am nothing. I pray God to kill me in some horrible manner."

In the monastery of La Sisla in Toledo lived a friar Alfonso de Toledo, a second-generation Converso whose father had come over to the True Faith in 1391. Friar Alfonso became a monk because he just did not know what else to do. But from the beginning God chastised him with a stabbing guilt for the terrible thing he had done. Twice he left the monastery to run far away. Both times his courage failed him and he came crawling back to beg forgiveness of his superiors and to lacerate his soul with meditations on the ancient Maccabees who had died gloriously for the Law of Moses. He would seek out the Jewish janitors when they came to clean, following after them and plucking at their sleeves to tell them he was really one of them at heart. He too loved only the Law of Moses, and he envied them for living honestly in their own faith. He begged them to call him Jacob, after his grandfather, and to flee the country with him, for he did not know how to go about it by himself. When the Inquisition came to Toledo and began burning Judaizing Conversos, he envied the victims as martyrs blessed in the sight of Jehovah. But, much as he wished that he too could be saved through martyrdom, he could not face the horror of the necessary preliminaries. So he fled, this time for good, to live with the greater tortures he carried in his head.

From the same monastery came another Converso friar, Juan de Madrid, a man so compulsively bold that he seemed to be deliberately seeking martyrdom. He boasted that he was really a Jew, was proud of it, and that for every Mosaic rule he followed he broke three Christian ones. He became a friar because that was the best way to practice Judaism. In the solitude of the monastery he would be shielded from the prying eyes of the Christian public. Besides, he could use the power of the confessional to lead penitents into Mosaic practices. He scorned to flee when the Inquisitors arrived in Toledo. He cursed them openly and from his confessional booth announced to sinners that it was a mortal sin to approve of the Inquisition. As he must have expected, friar Juan was one of the first to be denounced and was burned at the stake.

However the Jews themselves felt toward the guilt-ridden Converso, they must have been horrified at the behavior of their former colleagues who now became their persecutors. Whatever their reasons—which I am confident everyone can explain to his own satisfaction—some Conversos were determined to wipe out all reminders of their past. Back in the early fourteenth century a learned Jew named Abner of Burgos was reborn as a Christian at the age of sixty. Under his new name of Alfonso de Valladolid he devoted his remaining fourteen years to a long series of tracts against the Jews which earned him a certain historical fame (usually in footnote form) as an early champion of anti-Semitism in Spain. A few years before the Massacres of 1391, Peter IV of Aragon had to restrain some recent converts from making sallies into the ghetto at Mallorca, where they insisted on preaching to their former Jewish friends and stirring up a general ruckus when the Jews failed to respond sympathetically to their exhortations.

In the fifteenth century this sort of work acquired a professional status which was greatly enhanced by the special authority people attach to the revelations of the reformed ex-enemy now working for our side. Joshua Lorca, former rabbi and wise in the ways of the Talmud, was transformed by baptism into Jerome of the Holy Faith (Geronimo de Santa Fe). He offered his services to Pope Benedict XIII[1] as personal physician and dialectical wizard against the rabbis. Benedict sponsored a Great Debate at Tortosa in northern Spain in which Geronimo proved, against the arguments of the leading rabbis of Spain, that Jesus Christ was the True Messiah. The accounts of this "debate," recorded by eye witnesses and contemporaries among the Faithful, call to mind another favorite Spanish pastime—the Bullfight. The game was rigged in favor of the Matador. The fourteen rabbis summoned into the ring were warned by the pope that he would not tolerate any nonsense.

> *You, the most learned of the Hebrews,* (he said) *know ye that I am not here in this place, nor have I convened you here to debate whether our religion or yours is the true one. You are here only for Geronimo de Santa Fe who will prove to you that the coming of the Messiah was verified long centuries ago, availing himself of your own Talmud, a book forged by men much more learned than you. Be careful, then, to debate only on this subject and no other.*

Christian dignitaries flocked to Tortosa from all over Spain and northern Europe. Geronimo, aided by the rightness of his cause, demolished the feeble arguments of the rabbis in sixty nine logic-chopping sessions, to the universal edification of the entire company and of twelve of the fourteen rabbis, who were converted to the True Faith by the inspired eloquence of their former colleague.

Geronimo followed up his victory at Tortosa with a missionary tour of the northern provinces. A report to the king of Aragon tells of the wondrous preachings of Geronimo, "illuminated by

---

[1] At this moment (1413) there were three popes, resulting from a long series of follies generally dignified under the name of "conflicting political interests." Spain supported Benedict, who guarded the heavenly gates at Avignon in the south of France.

the Holy Spirit." He has made many conversions among the Jews, and the only holdouts have been among persons "of little worth." Even so, the report continues, "we have confidence in our Savior Jesus Christ that they too will come to salvation in a few days." The report concludes with a Scriptural observation about a shepherd and some lost sheep. Some years later Geronimo de Santa Fe summed up his career in a book—*The Scourge of the Hebrews*[1]—exposing the lewdness and subversions of the Talmud.

Other Conversos kept up the literary drumfire against the Jews. Pedro de la Caballeria, in his *Zeal of Christ against the Jews, Saracens and Infidels*,[2] maintained that the welfare of Christianity required the destruction in its midst of the "synagogue of Satan" and, of course, of Moors and other infidels. Bishop Paul of Saint Mary (Pablo de Santa Maria)—formerly Rabbi Solomon Halevi —after a careful scrutiny of Scripture,[3] concluded that the Jews were a menace and the Massacres of 1391 had been fashioned by the hand of God.

The undisputed leader of this inverted crusade was Alonso de Espina, former rabbi turned Franciscan friar. He was a violent blend of his predecessor Ferdinand Martinez, his contemporary Vincent Ferrer, and Thomas de Torquemada who was only one short generation behind him. Like Martinez he preached holy extermination; like Ferrer he thrust the Gospel on stiff-necked Jews, and like Torquemada he called for an Inquisition to purge the Conversos.

Espina's great masterwork was his *Fortress of the Faith*,[4] published in 1459. From the European rubble heaps of Christian hatred and murder, friar Alonso sifted out all the popular legends about Jews who murder Christian children, set fire to Christian houses, put hexes on Christian churches, stab Communion wafers

---

[1] *Hebraeomastix.*
[2] *Tractatus zelus Christi contra Judaeos, Sarracenos et infideles.*
[3] *Scrutinium Scripturarum.*
[4] *Fortalicium Fidei.*

THE REIGN OF ANTICHRIST. (From a 15th century engraving.)

and flog crucifixes, abominate holy images, vomit ritual blasphemies on the Savior and the Apostles and poison the Christian water supply.

For every Christian he cures the Jewish physician kills fifty others, and he holds regular meetings with the other devils of his trade where they tally up the numbers of their victims in testimony of their obedience to Jewish Law which commands them to slay True Believers. They are waiting only for the coming of the Antichrist to lead them against the Godly. Deep in the bowels of the Caspian Mountains, behind a magic wall, between the castles of Gog and Magog, waits a vast army of Jews which has been growing since the time of the ancient world. They will form the vanguard in the legions of Antichrist, their promised Messiah, when he comes to grind down the enemies of Israel and restore the world to the Jews.

There is a great deal more but I see no need to muck about in such a cesspool any longer than is necessary to catch its odor. It is, however, instructive though depressing to note that some historians' judgments are so hedged in by a mechanistic objectivity that they consider it "prejudice" to describe friar Alonso for what he was—a homicidal zealot preaching mass murder.

For a few happy years the Converso seemed to have the world in his palm. Now he was about to get his comeuppance. Friar Alonso, though a Converso himself, damned the Conversos as Jews at heart, worming their way into high posts to deceive princes and prelates, meanwhile practicing Jewish rites in secret and awaiting the coming of the Antichrist to throw off their disguise and join in the slaughter of the Faithful. This chant was quickly taken up by the Old Christians, who needed no urging. Besides, they were better qualified than friar Alonso to exalt the virtues of racial purity.

CHAPTER 5

Traitors to the Faith

IN 1450, when friar Alonso was still collecting material for his *Fortress of the Faith*, a Spanish cardinal at the papal court of Nicholas V published in Rome a vigorous denunciation of his countrymen's treatment of the New Christians.[1] The year before, mobs in Toledo had protested a new tax levy by running amuck and killing Conversos in sufficient quantity to compensate for the indignity to their pocketbooks. Such actions, wrote the cardinal, recalled the atrocities perpetrated against Israel by the ancient Midianities and Ishmaelites. Those responsible were "ministers of the Devil and enemies of God." Their behavior was irrational, unjust, malicious; it was inspired by hate, vengeance and greed; they were impious, sacrilegious, blasphemous and diabolical.

The cardinal also took note of the growing popular view that the Converso's Jewish blood guaranteed his wickedness and hatred of the True Faith. This was an impious contradiction of Scripture itself: the Savior Himself, the Blessed Virgin, all the early saints, and in fact all the ancient pillars of the True Faith carried the blood of Abraham and Moses in their veins. Christianity knows no distinctions of race; it does not persecute a man for his ancestry.

---

[1] *Tractatus contra Madianitas et Ismaelitas.*

The Converso, baptised into the True Faith, accepting its teachings and acknowledging its unique truth, is a legitimate member of the Holy, Apostolic and Universal Church and should be accepted as such by anyone who pretends to the name of Christian.

The most surprising thing about this book is that it was written by Juan de Torquemada, uncle of the future Inquisitor General. The least surprising thing is that the author's sentiments were completely out of tune with those of his countrymen back home. Alonso de Espina's ravings about the Antichrist in Converso disguise represented the considered judgment of both ignoramus and intellectual that the New Christian class of Spain was the breeding ground for the Devil's final campaign against Christianity. This opinion was shared outside Spain as well. We have already seen, for example, how Europeans generally traced the Black Death to the machinations of Mosaic wizards in the Spanish ghettos. A century later, while Cardinal Torquemada was vainly hurling his admonitions against the winds of popular hatred, a French chronicler identified the Antichrist as a Spanish Converso.

In the present year of 1445 (wrote Mathieu d'Escouchy) *there came to France a learned young man of twenty five, who claimed to be a native of Spain. He was of medium height, good appearance, very pleasant with all those with whom he came in contact, and he had the most profound knowledge ever seen anywhere in all the sciences, and especially in ecclesiastical matters. He was also a skilful knight-at-arms and a Doctor in theology, medicine, and the laws. He knew more about music than anybody else, playing all instruments superbly and explaining the rules and procedures for each one. He was also a swordsman without parallel. After traveling through many parts of this kingdom he came to Paris, where in the presence of forty or fifty of the most eminent men of the University, he was examined and questioned in various branches of learning, and he replied with such learning and sound reasoning that nobody could find anything which needed correcting. He also appeared before the Parlement of Paris and in other assemblages, without finding anyone who could successfully oppose him. He remained some time in Paris and then went to Ghent with the intention of visiting the court of the Duke of Burgundy. There also he was examined by the most learned men, who judged him to be without equal.*

After the departure of this young prodigy, the leading savants of the University of Paris met to ponder on his wonders. In solemn discussion they came to the inescapable conclusion that no human being, even if he lived to be a hundred, could possibly possess the knowledge exhibited by the young wizard from Spain. Obviously then, he was not a human being, and the learned doctors of Paris delivered themselves of the following considered judgment.

Their recent visitor was either the Antichrist himself or one of his lieutenants, and acquired his fabulous knowledge by black magic. This conclusion was further substantiated by the scholarly findings of those who specialized in Antichrist research. The Antichrist would be born in time of war.[1] He would be the offspring of an adulterous arrangement between a Christian man and a Converso woman. He would be possessed by the Devil, whose vast knowledge he would acquire. Posing as a Christian during his youth he would visit the nations of Europe to confound them with his learning. At the age of twenty-eight he would go to Jerusalem where the Jews would receive him as their God. There he would reign until the age of thirty-two, practicing such great cruelty and persecutions that God our Creator would destroy him with a firebolt from Heaven and this would signal the end of the world.

Apocalyptic tales about Antichrists and Judgment Day have always had a tingling fascination for the popular mind. Usually, however, except for a few enthusiasts who take to building arks or to twenty-four hour prayer sessions in isolated huts on the prairie, most people refuse to allow tomorrow's doom to intrude on today's practical problems of existence. The Spaniard undoubtedly believed these popular tales about the Antichrist and his murdering

---

[1] The Hundred Years' War between France and England was in its final stages.

legions, and all the talk about thunderbolts, cosmic trumpet blasts and the world rolling up like a scroll must have sent a delicious chill of fear through his veins. It also added a transcendental flavor to his everyday earthbound hatred of the Jews, and it was this latter sentiment which ultimately accounts for everything else.

In 1391 and the years immediately following, Christian hatred of the Jew focussed on the latter's rejection of the True Faith. Once the Jews accepted baptism, so it was believed, the Jewish "problem" would disappear. But the "problem" did not disappear; in fact—disregarding for the moment those who remained steadfast in the faith of Moses—the "problem" became steadily more intense. The usual explanation is that many Conversos were waxing fat on their new Christian freedoms while secretly adhering to their old faith and even raising their children in it. They were therefore hypocrites and deceivers, publicly pretending to be Christians but too cowardly to face the consequences of their religious beliefs.

It is perfectly true that many Conversos practiced just such deceptions, and both Christian and Jewish historians have criticised them for it. But what were their alternatives? They chose baptism as a lesser evil than death. They still believed in the truth of their ancient religion. To return to that religion meant death at the stake. A few, as we have seen, took that risk. Others, whose religious sentiments were adaptable to changing circumstances, made the most of their new found opportunities. The great majority, however, tried to make the best of an intolerable situation. Their "crime" lay in their inability to accept a belief thrust upon them by their persecutors and in their reluctance to die a martyr's death. The former is a crime only for those who look upon convictions as exchangeable merchandise; the latter can only offend those who demand martyrdom in others as the price of their approval.

Modern anti-Semitism has nothing to do with the Jewish religion. In fact it has nothing really to do with the Jew at all. He can be poor, rich, Christian, Jew, atheist, conservative, radical, garbage man or international banker. He is still a Jew because the anti-Semite would be desolate without him. At what point "Jewishness" became a necessary reality for the sustenance of the sick is probably impossible to say. Perhaps it was such a reality from Old Testament times, serving the apparently universal need of man for someone he can kick with impunity.

In any case, the first external signs that anti-Semitism in Spain was taking on a "racial" rather than an exclusively "religious" cast, appear in these years of the middle fifteenth century. An Old Christian contemporary of Alonso de Espina summed up the new thesis that any Converso was no more than a filthy Jew in Christian disguise:

> ... *the despised, damned and detested generation of baptised Jews and all those descended from their accursed lineage, adulterers sunk in disbelief and infidelity, fathers of all greed, sowers of all discord and division, abounding in malice and perverseness, eternal ingrates against God, violaters of His commandments, deviators from His ways.*

Another writer used the "comedy" touch to make the same point and also to add a few Jewish personality traits which will be familiar to the modern reader. The author employs the elaborate literary device of an imaginary grant by the king to an Old Christian nobleman, conferring on him the title of Converso. The reason, as our unknown author explains with elephantine levity, is to allow the Old Christian nobleman to enjoy all the rights and privileges of the pushy Conversos, "recently hatched among us because of our sins." The honest Old Christian is hereby empowered to use all the "subtleties, arts, double-dealings and deceptions" of the Conversos. He may deceive and trick pure Christians with flattery and hypocrisy; he may buy his way into the priesthood to learn their sins in the confessional and report them to the authorities. He may also buy a public office and fasten his hooks into honest people. He may become a physician so he can kill good Christians, take over their widows and property and foul the purity of their blood. And so on, and on, and on.

The distinction between Jew and Converso was legally a very important one, but in the public mind all other distinctions were rapidly disappearing. In his *History of the Catholic Kings* (Ferdinand and Isabella), the popular historian Andres Bernaldez describes the "circumstances" which led to the establishment of the Spanish Inquisition. His analysis of causes is open to debate but his sentiments[1] clearly reflect the new image of the Converso as a Jew in disguise and, incidentally, of the evolving concept of the Jew as a racial "problem."

Bernaldez traces the Mosaic heresy parading under the name of Christianity back to the Massacres of 1391. It began then and continued to grow secretly ever since until it had spread into all the corners of the realm: "Oh wild and damnable bestiality, evil nourished by treason." As for the Jews who kept their faith, they are gluttons feeding on garbage fried in oil. Their houses "stink vilely" from their cooking. Their bodies also stink because they eat onions and garlic, and also because they have not been baptised.

The Conversos, although they have been baptised, stink just like the Jews because they still believe in the Jewish faith. They pretend to be Christians, of course, because it is profitable for them to do so. But they still do not like pork and they are never reluctant to eat meat during Lent. They keep the Passover and the Jewish Sabbath; they secretly invite rabbis to their homes to preach to them and slaughter their meat and poultry in the Jewish fashion. They seek whenever possible to avoid the sacraments of the Holy Church. They never confess their sins; they do not fear

---
[1] Bernaldez, the "priest of Los Palacios," was born about 1450 and died about 1514. His *History* is an excellent source for both the events and the popular sentiments of this period. He took a great interest in the religious problem and was an eyewitness to many of the Jewish misfortunes of the later fifteenth century. Unlike most historians, who write for a reasonably learned posterity, Bernaldez prided himself on being a spokesman of the masses and a reflector of the views of the common man, even to the point of writing in his language. For both these reasons we shall have occasion to hear from him more often as we move closer to Torquemada who, unfortunately, kept most of his thoughts to himself.

excommunication; they blaspheme against the Savior and the Apostles. Not without reason did our Lord call them a wicked and adulterous generation. For they disdain virginity and chastity, seeking only to multiply. They buy their way into monasteries. They ravish nuns, swindle honest people, and steal and lie without conscience. They disdain to work with their hands, to dig the soil or work the fields, to plough and till or raise cattle. Instead, they work only at the easiest jobs where they can make the most money with as little labor as possible.

The anti-Semitism of Bernaldez is an extension of a "racial" philosophy which began to take shape after the Massacres of 1391 and the subsequent growth of the New Christian class. In the latter sixteenth century purity of blood became a test of public office in Spain, and by the seventeenth century the "racial" theory was firmly established on the principle that a twentieth part—indeed the merest trace—of Jewish blood was conclusive evidence of one's natural inferiority to his Christian neighbors.

However, the fifteenth-century mind had not reached this degree of anthropological sophistication and still hoped to solve its Jewish "problem" by religious purification. The Jewish community was being whittled down by a policy of legal and extra-legal attrition and if that should fail, perhaps sterner measures could be found. But the Converso was a Christian and however suspect his enthusiasm for the True Faith, there was no effective way to deal with him on a legal basis. Yet, as the anonymous author of the *Chronicle of Don Alvaro de Luna* wrote in 1455, "against these heretics and bad Christians we must wage even more merciless war than against the most notorious of infidels." Unfortunately, the battalions of orthodoxy were pitifully inadequate. In Aragon the old Roman Inquisition exerted only a desultory authority; in Castile, where the local bishops had jurisdiction over heresy, there were occasional burnings of Judaizing Conversos. Sporadic outbursts of mob violence against New Christians also helped the cause. But the Enemy was powerful and alert, and he used his influence in high places to thwart these scattered efforts to destroy him.

Friar Alonso de Espina, as might be expected, initiated the first serious efforts to establish a local Inquisition to pursue the Judaizing Converso on a systematic basis. In a letter to the General of the Geronomite order, Espina and his Franciscan colleagues called for a joint effort to persuade Henry IV of Castile to establish an Inquisition in that kingdom. The growing influence of the Conversos demanded quick action by the clergy before it was too late:

> *And now we—who occupy the places of the saints here on earth, and who should be an example of light to the world—see the unbelievers growing and heretics destroying and subverting the Faith of Jesus Christ while we sit silently by.*

An Inquisition, friar Alonso maintained, would separate the good Conversos (like himself) from the bad; it would protect the Holy Faith from corruption and restore peace and honor to the realm.

Contemporary accounts tell us that this proposal produced "an extraordinary effect" on the Geronomites. They addressed numerous prayers to God beseeching His assistance; they shed copious tears over the corrosion of Converso souls and they convoked a general council to consider the problem. Meanwhile, the impatient Franciscans addressed an appeal directly to King Henry. Unfortunately, the king allowed himself to be sidetracked by the claim of one of the friars that he had a collection of Converso foreskins to prove that the New Christians were still practicing Judaism. When the king demanded to see them the friar stammered something to the effect that it was somebody else who was collecting foreskins but he didn't know who it was. As for the Geronomites, they apparently dried their tears and concluded that Alonso de Espina and his friends had gone too far. The only satisfaction the Franciscans got was a half-hearted declaration by

King Henry in 1464 deploring the spread of Judaism among the Conversos of Castile and directing the local bishops to root it out. A few burnings followed this announcement, but nobody in authority seemed to be very enthusiastic about it and matters were soon back to normal. The frustrated crusaders would have to wait until Henry's death and the subsequent unification of the Spanish kingdoms under Ferdinand and Isabella before the work of purification could get under way in earnest. If they could have seen into the future they would have been content to wait, for the happy day was not far off.

CHAPTER 6

The Inquisition

ON OCTOBER 19, 1469, Prince Ferdinand, heir to the throne of Aragon, married the Princess Isabella, heiress to the throne of Castile. The importance of this union was fully appreciated by their contemporaries. It promised the unification of the Spanish world under the two greatest kingdoms of the Peninsula. It also promised a final solution to the problem of the Jew and Converso, but nobody seemed to be sure what form the solution would take. For example, among those who favored the marriage and the political stability it promised, were Isabella's confessor Thomas de Torquemada, and her adviser in secular matters, the Jew Abraham Seneor. As Isabella's spiritual tutor, Torquemada had for years impressed on her the need for purifying the realm of Judaism, both overt and in disguise. It was rumored that he had even extorted a promise from the young Isabella that when she became queen she would do all in her power to erase the stain of Judaism forever.

For his part, Abraham Seneor had quite different hopes of a Jewish future under Ferdinand and Isabella. There were many aspirants to the hand of Isabella, and Abraham Seneor used his great influence as royal favorite to help her pick the right partner. His choice fell on Ferdinand of Aragon because, it was said, the

THE INQUISITION

latter's alleged Converso background might leaven Isabella's religious enthusiasms sufficiently to avoid disaster for the Jews.

The history of the previous century clearly favored the designs of Torquemada and his friends, and the common people themselves apparently sensed the final victory also. Friar Alonso de Espina had recently passed to his reward, but a new generation, sprung from the bowels of Archdeacon Ferdinand Martinez mounted the pulpits to do his work. During the five years between Isabella's marriage and her accession to the throne of Castile the traditions of 1391 were revived, this time against the hated Converso. It started, appropriately, in Valladolid, where the royal nuptials had taken place. In 1470 the mob fell upon the New Christians of that city and subsided only when royal troops were dispatched to the scene to restore order. Two years later southern Spain was afire. A religious procession in Cordova was disrupted when someone emptied a vessel of unidentified liquid out of a window and the contents splashed on a canopy which sheltered a picture of the Blessed Virgin. Immediately the cry arose that the culprit was a Converso, the liquid was not water and this was no accident.

For three days the enraged citizenry of Cordova killed Conversos, plundered and then burned their homes, and rudely manhandled the local authorities who tried to stop the slaughter. Even the presence of the great aristocrat Don Alonso de Aguilar failed to cow them; after being vigorously pelted with stones Don Alonso prudently withdrew to the safety of his castle.

From Cordova the slaughter spread to other towns in Andalusia where the Conversos sought refuge. An eyewitness of these events reports that

> *of those who escaped, many went to the town of Palma. Others went to Ecija and Jerez and anywhere else they could secure refuge from the local governors. In Adamuz and in Montoro and in La Rambla they were robbed and severely manhandled. In Almodovar del Campo some of the Conversos were robbed and killed by the peasants.*

The refugees in Palma, near Seville, applied to the local governor, the duke of Medina-Sidonia, for permission to take refuge in Gibraltar, offering the duke a yearly income of considerable size in return for his generosity. The duke's advisers heartily disapproved: the Conversos were too lazy, too useless and too unworthy to settle in Gibraltar. The duke, however, refused to listen and accepted the offer. But he reckoned without the Voice of the People, who began turning Seville upside down when they heard of their duke's folly. It was now the turn of the Conversos of Seville. Some of them sought the doubtful safety of other towns; some went to Flanders and Italy, never to return. Those who stayed buried their valuables in caves and locked themselves inside the walls of the ancient Jewish quarter, determined to resist to the death as their ancestors had done in 1391. The final assault did not come in 1473, but the Conversos of Seville could not know that a more inexorable fate was just ahead.

Ferdinand and Isabella visited Segovia in 1474, a few days after a massacre of Conversos there. The walls of the houses were still spotted with fresh blood and the city was threatened with disease from the corpses rotting in the streets. For the Catholic Kings such a state of affairs was too politically untidy to be tolerated for very long. At the moment, however, the more pressing problem of their own royal survival diverted their attention from religious and racial matters. The death of Isabella's half-brother Henry IV in 1475 brought on a disputed succession and fitful civil war which absorbed all the queen's attention for the next five years. But by 1480 Prince Ferdinand had succeeded his father as king of Aragon and Isabella had crushed her opposition and thrust her rival for the throne into a Portuguese convent.

During these uncertain years, pious prelates and Old Christians had been breaking the queen's ears with their exhortations for an Inquisition against the Conversos. How much Torquemada had to say in the privacy of the royal chamber we simply do not know, but the credit—if that is the word—for the actual creation of the Spanish Inquisition must go to another: friar Alonso de Ojeda of the Dominican monastery of San Pablo in Seville. For several years Ojeda dogged the royal footsteps carrying tales about the spreading Converso infection and the need for immediate action if Spain were to be saved. The queen was wavering. It was time for a Jewish horror story, and Ojeda was not a man to shirk his responsibilities. In 1487 he hastened from Seville to the royal court at Cordova to reveal a horrifying discovery. An amorous Christian of the pure blood was carrying on an informal romance with a pretty Jewess in the ghetto of Seville. During the Easter week just past he had seen a group of Conversos and Jews doing strange things in his sweetheart's home. He was not very clear as to just what these things were, but Ojeda knew: the Conversos of Seville were celebrating Holy Week with their Jewish brethren by practicing ritual abominations against Christianity and its Founder.

Ferdinand and Isabella were scandalized. "The king and queen were very upset and pained to discover that there were people in their lands who felt badly about the Christian religion," one contemporary reports. The Spanish ambassador in Rome was instructed to negotiate with the Pope for the creation of a special Inquisition for Spain. November 1, 1478, Sixtus IV issued a bull recording the papal displeasure with false Christians and authorizing the establishment of the Spanish Inquisition. After the customary delays inherent in all administrative machinery, the Catholic Kings issued a lengthy proclamation setting up the first Inquisition tribunal in Seville September 27, 1480.

In our kingdoms (they declared) *there are some bad Christians, both men and women, who are apostates and heretics. Although they have been baptised in the True Faith they bear only the name and appearance of Christians, for they daily return to the superstitions and perfidious sect of the Jews. Scornful of the Holy Mother church, they have allowed themselves to incur the sentence of censure and excommunication, together with other penalties established by the Apostolic laws and constitutions. Not only have they persisted in their blind and obstinate heresy, but their children and descendants do likewise, and those who treat with them also are stained by that same infidelity and heresy.*

This is familiar language, of course, but this time it was a preface to grim action. Inspired by the greatest desire and zeal for the Faith, to secure the well-being of the Faithful on earth and in Heaven, and to exalt virtue by abasing the wicked, their majesties herewith appointed two Dominican friars—Miguel de Morillo and Juan de San Martin—as Inquisitors and defenders of the Holy Faith against the machinations of the Conversos of Seville.

Headquarters for the Inquisition tribunal were in Ojeda's monastery of San Pablo, which seems fitting. Ojeda was also chosen to preach the ceremonial sermon at the first Auto de Fe celebrated by the new Inquisition. Almost immediately afterward, he died of the plague, and we can imagine that friend and enemy alike saw in this the workings of Providence.

Even before the Inquisitors began operations, many Conversos fled Seville to take refuge on the hereditary lands of the nearby nobility, particularly those of the marquis of Cadiz, whose influence and rank promised a certain immunity from the obedience demanded of ordinary men. The marquis perhaps had his own selfish reasons for allowing these refugees to settle within his dominions, but the fact that he did so also demonstrates a principle evident in the earlier history of the Spanish crusade against Judaism. The uncompromising character of the Jewish pogrom came, not from the aristocracy, but from the Common People. This may violate the modern myth that the Common People are by some instinct of nature the only source of freedom, tolerance and general virtue, and that aristocracy is inherently wicked and cruel. But without launching into a disquisition on the merits or demerits of aristocracy, we feel safe in saying that for uncontrolled violence and pitiless persecution there is nothing in the bloody

THE INQUISITION

record of human history to equal the ferocity of the Common People once they have been stung into action.

The marquis quickly discovered that nobody was to be allowed to frustrate the authority of the Inquisition, and it becomes quite clear that Ferdinand and Isabella, in creating the Inquisition, were motivated by a mixture of both piety and political sagacity.[1] Certainly one of the reasons for establishing the Inquisition was to substitute the controlled force of authority for the uncontrolled violence of the People in dealing with religious affairs. Both Ferdinand and Isabella had a keen enough sense of history to wish to avoid the subversion of authority implicit in the mob actions of 1391 and after. They were equally alert to the dangers of allowing any assertion of independence by the grandees of the realm. Of this danger too, they had personal experience. The years immediately following their accession were taken up with the task of reducing the great nobility to submission and centralizing the authority of the realm in their own hands. It was to this problem that they turned first, even at the expense of having to delay the solution of the religious problem. Although this might have frustrated Ojeda and Torquemada, in the long run it had the effect of making the Inquisition, when it finally did come, an all-powerful institution and guaranteed success where earlier half-hearted and haphazard efforts had failed. Now the Crown was strong enough to purify the realm in an orderly, legal fashion. Unauthorized mob violence against Conversos was sternly punished as subversive of the authority of the Crown. And unauthorized asylum for Conversos would be treated precisely the same way for precisely the same reason.

Consequently, when it became apparent that the marquis of

---

[1] Tradition assigns the piety to Isabella and the political sagacity to Ferdinand, whom Machiavelli praised as the cunning fox. However, the sarcophagus of the Catholic Kings in Granada represents Ferdinand lying with his head on an undented pillow, whereas Isabella's head makes an impressive dent in hers. The natives take pleasure in pointing this out as evidence of Isabella's intellectual superiority, but we may safely attribute the discrepancy to the loyal prejudice of a Castilian sculptor.

THE CASTLE OF TRIANA IN SEVILLE, HEADQUARTERS OF THE INQUISITION.

Cadiz and other grandees of the realm were presuming to receive refugee Conversos on their lands, the two Inquisitors at Seville took immediate action. January 2, 1481, they delivered themselves of a strongly worded proclamation which had all the force of the Crown behind it. The marquis and others like him were ordered to seize all refugee Conversos in their dominions and deliver them forthwith to the Inquisitors of Seville. Failure to comply would mean excommunication, as well as confiscation of all lands and noble perquisites, and Inquisitorial prosecution as protectors of heretics. Contemporaries report that thousands of such refugees were returned and the detention rooms at the monastery became so overcrowded that the Inquisitors were forced to move into larger quarters in the great Castle of Triana just outside the walls of Seville.

A few of the Conversos apparently decided to resist, although the story of the Seville conspiracy against the Inquisition is so clouded in murky romance that the details fail to come through. The general outline of the second-hand accounts which have come down to us goes something like this: a handful of wealthy Conversos in Seville began meeting secretly at night to plan an uprising against the Inquisition. There was some talk about tyrants, hidden weapons and the virtues of assassinating Inquisitors. It all came to naught when the beautiful—the wondrously beautiful—daughter of one of the leading conspirators confided the news to her Old Christian lover. The latter raced to tell the Inquisitors, the plotters were rounded up in the well-worn nick of time and were burned at the stake in the first Auto de Fe, to the accompaniment of an appropriately indignant sermon by friar Alonso de Ojeda. The beautiful daughter escaped this grisly fate only to spin out a life of remorse and disintegration reminiscent of the later career of Lady Hamilton.

A certain weariness prevents us from recording in detail the thousands of trials which took place during these initial Inquisitorial years. Autos de Fe became a regular feature of life in Seville, with great parades of penitents, elaborate purification ceremonies, exciting sermons, and finally the burning alive of the gravest offenders. Those who had managed to escape were burned in effigy. The bones of the dead were dug up, solemnly tried, and burned. Thousands of the frightened living came forward voluntarily to confess their guilt under a promise of mercy and to denounce their neighbors as secret Judaizers. As the trials proceeded, the existence of a vast Judaizing conspiracy throughout Spain became more horrifyingly apparent to the Old Christian Faithful.

The historian Bernaldez accurately recorded the general sentiment of the age.

> *In Seville* (he writes) *it was learned that the Conversos of Cordova, Toledo, Burgos, Valencia, Segovia, and all of Spain, were all Jews and held to the same hope which the people of Israel had in Egypt: that although they were persecuted by the Egyptians God would lead them out of Egypt as He later did with His strong hand and extended arm. And thus the Jews look upon the Christians as Egyptians, or worse, and believe that God will miraculously sustain and defend them and that they will be led by the hand of God from among the Christians and into the Promised land. In this manner they live and remain among Christians, entertaining these mad hopes as they have confessed at their trials, thus making it clear that their whole race is defamed and infected by this sickness. It is impossible to describe the wickedness of this heretical depravity. I can only say that now that the fires are lit they will burn until this pestilence is destroyed root and branch if they have to burn until every Judaizer is consumed to death and no more remain.*

To expand the operations begun in Seville, the Catholic Kings obtained early in 1482 a papal bull naming eight new Inquisitors for Spain. Meanwhile the Crown set about reorganizing the Inquisition machinery for the more effective prosecution of heresy. In 1483 they created a new royal council of the Supreme and General Inquisition to expand the operations begun at Seville. At the head of this council they placed the royal confessor Thomas de Torquemada, with the title of Inquisitor General of Spain. The work of purification was now to begin on a thorough scale.

CHAPTER 7

Inquisitor General Torquemada

FEW MEN HAVE BEEN SO COMPLETELY in tune with their age as was Thomas de Torquemada. Yet, though his name symbolizes his age, details about his life are extremely scarce. We are not even certain of his place or date of birth. We do know, however, that he grew up in Valladolid and, like his uncle (Cardinal Juan de Torquemada) he entered the Lord's service through the local Dominican monastery of San Pablo. On completion of his training in Valladolid he was sent to the Dominican house at Piedrahita, a small town near Avila.[1] There, it is said, he earned a solid

---

[1] Piedrahita enjoyed a momentary fame about fifty years later as the home of a visionary lady who confounded her contemporaries in the early sixteenth century. The daughter of a local peasant, she became a tertiary sister (*beata*) in the Dominican order in Piedrahita, taking the name of Maria de Santo Domingo. Maria was gifted with numerous revelations, in which she held celestial converse with the Blessed Virgin and the Savior. She informed her contemporaries that Christ was with her, that she was Christ, and that she was Christ's bride. For hours she would remain in an ecstatic trance, unmoving, her arms and legs rigidly extended, dissolving herself in the arms of the Deity. Though unlearned she was reputed to be the equal of the most sophisticated theologians, her supernatural lights easily compensating for her lack of schooling. Some of these theologians, however, suspected that she was inspired by the devil rather than God, and serious charges were made regarding her orthodoxy. But King Ferdinand and the episcopal hierarchy were convinced that she enjoyed a special inspiration available to very few, and their support was largely responsible for the failure of Maria's critics to bring about her downfall as a heretic.

El Greco's "The Inquisitor General."

reputation for the triple virtues of learning, piety and austerity. As a result, he was chosen in 1452—in his very early thirties—as prior of the monastery of Santa Cruz at Segovia. Here he apparently first came in contact with the young Princess Isabella and accepted the obligation of confessing her on a fairly regular basis. He was undoubtedly present at Isabella's coronation in Segovia in 1474 and from that date his movements are largely determined by those of his queenly penitent. In 1483 he became Spain's first Inquisitor General and how devotedly he performed his duties we shall soon see. Fifteen years later, in his late seventies, he died at the Dominican monastery of Avila, which he had founded.

It is said that Torquemada wore a hair-shirt, refused to eat meat, wear linen garments or sleep between linen sheets or allow his sister to choose marriage over the nunnery. It is also said that he lived in palaces, that he surrounded himself with a princely retinue of two hundred fifty armed guards on foot and ahorse, that he lived in constant fear of assassination and adorned his table with the horn of a unicorn as a sovereign remedy against poison. He is further reported to have accumulated vast wealth through property confiscations by the Inquisition and to have declined on numerous occasions the offers by his grateful queen of the archbishoprics of Seville and Toledo. Most of these assertions come from "prejudiced" historians who do not like Torquemada; except for the reports about his hair-shirt and his humility in the matter of high episcopal office, such stories are firmly rejected by his "impartial" defenders.

Perhaps the hand of Providence has erased much of the personal record of Torquemada's life in order to save us from the distractions of academic bookkeeping. For Torquemada's importance to history lies in his role as an archetype rather than an individual. He was not a rebel jousting with popular windmills. He was not a Reformer determined to recast the universe in the mold of his personal convictions. He was not the entrepreneur of anti-Semitism. He was not even the creator of its legal instrument, the Inquisition. He was a man of recognized talent and competence who could be trusted completely to devote himself to the effective execution of a program which represented his own deepest desires as well as those of his age.

Historians who are quick to condemn Torquemada as a unique vessel of Satan are as quickly admonished by alert defenders for their failure to understand him as a product of his times. We do, I think, have an obligation to try to understand the circumstances and the flavor of an age which creates a man's attitudes and shapes his destiny. But we do not therefore have to condone the result, unless we consider it a proper duty of the historian to abdicate the system of human values even about known facts. I sometimes feel that the modern friends of Torquemada—or of a John Calvin for that matter—use the fetish of objectivity as a shield to ward off criticism of the wayward actions of past party members. The process has been developed into a subtle little ritual: the attorney for the defense, in a disarmingly "reasonable" manner, "admits" that his client did indeed commit murder, and then pleads extenuating circumstances such as the "temper of the times" or, in the case of religious murder (by Christians only), certain idealistic intentions and noble goals which motivated the deed. The facts in this case compel me to confess [a] that I do not like Ferdinand Martinez, Vincent Ferrer, Alonso de Espina and Thomas de Torquemada, even though I might have behaved as they did were I not a product of this enlightened century, and [b] that I do not like the spirit of the age which made them and which they served with such obvious relish. I see no reason—not even in the expropriated name of God or Historical Objectivity—why I should excuse by a specious "neutrality" the practice of mass murder for Wrong Thinking, whether it happened only yesterday or five long centuries ago. As for Torquemada, the man himself was no worse and no better than the mass of his contemporaries, and I do not share the view of those critics who single him out as an aberration from the mythical norm of human goodness and virtue. The whole age was caught up in a wave of persecution and murder that even the dialectical puffing of that apologists' darling, Mr. G. K. Chesterton, cannot completely obscure.[1]

As an honest interpreter and efficient administrator of the popular will, Torquemada was superb. In the fifteen years of his reign the Spanish Inquisition grew from the single tribunal at Seville to a network of two dozen Holy Offices covering the four corners of the Peninsula and everything in between. Nobody, however important, was exempt from prosecution. The court historian, Gonzalo de Santa Maria, of the illustrious Converso family of Burgos, was tried for Judaism three times and finally died in prison. Priests and friars were burned at the stake, especially in Toledo where the Geronomite monastery of La Sisla was discovered to be a hotbed of Judaism. In Cordova the treasurer of the local cathedral was accused of hiding a Communion wafer in his shoe; the wafer began to bleed and bathed his foot in crimson, thus leading to his seizure by the Inquisition. He broke down under questioning and confessed that for years he had observed Jewish religious practices and was in the habit of making scornful observations about the Savior. He was burned at the stake and presumably descended into Hell to join his mistress who had been burned a few months before him.

Probably Torquemada's biggest game among the clergy was Pedro de Aranda, bishop of Calahorra and president of the council of Castile. Aranda, a Converso, somehow learned that Torquemada was preparing a case against him, so he fled to Rome where the Pope employed him as his ambassador to Venice and Master of the Sacred Palace. But Torquemada sent a fulsome dossier to His Holiness, highlighted by the following charges: Aranda held that the Mosaic Law was not entirely without merit; he omitted the words "Son and Holy Spirit" when reciting the "Our Father"; he

---

[1] In *Orthodoxy*, Chesterton tosses off one of his typical contrapuntal phrases to compare the virtues of Torquemada with the vices of Emile Zola: "Torquemada tortured people physically for the sake of moral truth. Zola tortured people morally for the sake of physical truth. But in Torquemada's time there was at least a system that could to some extent make righteousness and peace kiss each other."

ate meat on Good Friday; he questioned the value of indulgences except for the crass object of making money; he believed in Paradise but expressed doubts about Hell and Purgatory. On the Pope's order the bishop was deposed and degraded from his holy orders and thrown into the Castle of San Angelo where he died soon after.

Torquemada directed the Inquisition with a scrupulosity that overlooked nothing. One Maria Sanchez was seized in 1485 on the strength of an accusation that went back five years. When the Holy Office was first opened at Seville, Maria apparently wondered out loud that King Ferdinand had consented to it, being a Converso himself. He was very sensitive on that score, according to Maria, and once struck the queen when she threw his origin up to him. In another case a priest of Toledo was accused of having said twenty years before, when he was a boy, that the Communion wafer was only bread and not the Body of Christ. He denied the charge, even under vigorous torture, and for those who like to remind us that not everybody was burned at the stake, we may note that the culprit in this case was only sentenced to make public abjuration of his heresy at an Auto de Fe. A similar fate, decided on equally flimsy evidence, overtook Diego Sanchez, organist of the cathedral at Toledo. A former maid in Diego's house, on her way to the stake, made peace with her Maker by announcing that Diego had once sent oil and candles to the local synagogue. Diego denied he had ever done such a terrible thing; his accuser, he said, was a thief and a slut, who had once sworn revenge when Diego discharged her for illegal pregnancy. Diego's colleagues and neighbors testified to his spotless record of twenty five years' service in the Toledo cathedral, although one of the chaplains had some reservations about the orthodoxy of Diego's eating habits. Just in case, therefore, Diego was required to appear as a penitent and abjure his heresies in an Auto de Fe.

To help guard against the spread of heresy Torquemada also celebrated a number of book-burning festivals, especially of Hebrew Bibles and, after the final defeat of the Moors at Granada in

1492, of Arabic books also. As for the children of heretics, who were inevitably susceptible to infection, they were considered not to be responsible for their false beliefs until they reached the ages of twelve (for girls) and fourteen (for boys). After that they were held to be adults and fully accountable to the Inquisition, although they would be accorded special mercy if they spontaneously denounced their heretical parents. The children of heretics burned at the stake or imprisoned for life were to be handed over to proper Christians who would bring them up in the True Faith, safe from the snares of evil counsellors.

It was a capital offense to talk against the Holy Office. In 1483 an Old Christian nobleman, friend and beneficiary of the Pope himself, was burned at the stake as a "pertinacious negativist" for cursing the Inquisition. A complaining woman suffered the same fate for saying that the Inquisition was more interested in confiscating people's property than in saving their souls. Some of the prisoners freed by the Inquisition tried to save their reputations by claiming they were innocent and had only confessed to heresy under torture. Torquemada quickly put an end to this chicanery by an order in 1484 that such persons were to be considered as false converts and to be prosecuted as such, the penalty for false conversion being death at the stake.

The Pope had a few complaints to make too.[1] Early in 1482 he wrote to Ferdinand and Isabella that the Seville Inquisitors,

> *without observing juridical prescriptions, have detained many persons in violation of justice, punishing them by severe tortures and imputing to them, without foundation, the crime of heresy, and despoiling of their wealth those sentenced to death, in such form that a great number of them have come to the Apostolic See, fleeing from such excessive rigor and protesting their orthodoxy.*

---

[1] Nobody could question the Pope's orthodoxy or his zeal for the Faith, so the modern apologist explains away the Pope's complaints on the ground that heretical refugees from Spain deceived him with their lies about the Inquisition. The usually perceptive and well-informed pontiff in this unique instance becomes a naive Trilby to the Sephardic Svengalis who seek to obstruct the pious work of Torquemada.

A year later the Pope complained again. The Spanish Inquisitors, he said, appear to be more interested in confiscating people's wealth than in saving their souls. As a result they are even jailing, torturing and burning at the stake a number of innocent people whose property they then confiscate. More complaints of the same nature came from Rome in succeeding years, but Torquemada early made clear his position in the matter. In his "Instructions" to the tribunals in 1484 he refers to the papal complaints which would prejudice the free functioning of Inquisition justice and announces that no such obstacles must be allowed to interfere with the task of protecting the True Faith against those who seek to destroy it.

The worst skulduggery took place at home. The Conversos of Toledo, following the example of their kinsmen in Seville, concocted a plot to kill the local Inquisitors and raise a general rebellion in town, even to the point of defying the Crown. The conspiracy was discovered in the customary nick of time and the plotters were wiped out in an Auto de Fe. In Segovia, Bishop Juan Davila made no secret of his objections to the establishment of an agency of the Holy Office in his diocese. Though a Converso himself he had for years used his episcopal authority to harass Jews and burn Converso Judaizers, and he wanted neither help nor interference from the agents of Torquemada. The latter had no Inquisitorial authority over obstructive bishops so he began fattening up a dossier to be sent to Rome along with Bishop Davila. In addition to charges of aiding heresy by opposing the introduction of the Inquisition in Segovia, it included the allegation that the bishop had secretly dug up the bones of his ancestors (in the dead of night, of course) and hidden them from pious eyes seeking proof that they had been buried in the Jewish fashion. The bishop was finally sent off to Rome for trial at the papal court. The case dragged on for years and he died before its conclusion, which was inconclusive. In Segovia, meanwhile, the new Inquisition tribunal flourished without further hindrance.

The kingdom of Aragon jealously guarded its local privileges against encroachment by outsiders. Only after much heated debate did the national Cortes of Aragon finally consent in 1484 to the introduction of Torquemada's Inquisition. Even then, local resistance had to be overcome in a number of cities, Barcelona, Valencia, Teruel and Saragossa being the most difficult. In the latter place all the ugly forces of hate and violence came together in their most destructive form. The plot against the Holy Office in that city included some of the most eminent Conversos of the realm from the families of Santa Fe, Santa Maria, Caballeria, Santa Cruz and Santangel. The symbol of their hatred, and immediate object of their attention, was the local Inquisitor, Pedro Arbues.

Inquisitor Arbues apparently suspected that his enemies were bent on killing him, for he never appeared in public without an armed guard to protect him. The Conversos waited him out in the established tradition of Renaissance assassination, which was to catch the victim offguard in church. On the evening of September 15, 1485, Arbues was kneeling before the high altar in the cathedral at Saragossa when a professional assassin by the name of Durango stepped up behind him and struck him in the neck with a sword, "splitting him open from his cervix to his beard," as a contemporary put it. Arbues lurched about briefly while two other assassins stabbed him repeatedly through the body until he was dead.

Retribution was even more terrible than the deed. Hundreds of suspects were thrown into the dungeons of the Inquisition while the Holy Office pondered their fate. Those directly implicated were disposed of in a manner best calculated to slake the blood thirst of the enraged populace, as well as to discourage future assassinations of heavenly agents. The chief assassin—Durango—was hauled out to the great square; his hands were cut off and nailed to the door of the House of Deputies, while he was allowed to bleed to death. His body was then carted off to the market place where the head was detached, the trunk pulled apart by horses, and the pieces hung in the streets. One of his companions was burned alive, his hands being hacked off immediately prior to the lighting of the fire. The third assassin frustrated his captors by eating a glass lamp in his cell. His remains were brought out, however, and cut up into pieces while his wife, who unfortunately was still living, was burned alive as an accessory to the murder. For several years the vengeance continued as more details were wrung from the prisoners. The names of some of Spain's most illustrious Converso families appear on the lists of conspirators burned alive, in corpse, and in effigy in the great Autos de Fe which followed the assassination of Inquisitor Arbues. The most shocking, perhaps, is that of Francisco de Santa Fe, son of the great debater and missionary Geronimo de Santa Fe. Francisco died by hurling himself from his prison tower to avoid being burned alive. His broken corpse was burned, of course, for the inflicting of indignity was as important as death itself. In any event, there would be no more resistance to the new Inquisition and Torquemada could get on with his work.

CHAPTER 8

The Alboraico

WHAT, exactly, was a Judaizing heretic? At what point, and by what actions, did a professing Christian become an apostate from Truth? What were the signs by which his crime could be detected?

Theology, with all its dialectical refinements, had always been a special interest of the Dominican order. Most of the Inquisitors, like their general Torquemada, were Dominicans and therefore subtly sophisticated about heresy. Besides, since Christians and Jews had been partners in Spanish civilization for so many centuries they were bound to know a good deal about each other's religion.

At the outset, Torquemada provided his organization with one perfectly reliable source of information about backsliding Conversos. He ordered all the rabbis of Spain to denounce to the Inquisition any Conversos whom they knew to be practicing Judaism. The rabbis were also forced to announce to their congregations that under pain of excommunication from the synagogue all Jews must report to the Inquisition any Conversos who gave alms to the synagogue or who in any way whatsoever inclined to their ancestral faith. Excommunication for a Jew was as horrendous as it was for a Christian, and the mere threat brought forth a flock of denunciations to the Inquisition. A Jewish contemporary recorded that Torquemada's order resulted in the burning of "many thousands" and the confiscation of private fortunes "without number."

Some of the early Inquisition cases, however, suggest that the Inquisitors were not always sure about what properly constituted a Judaic heresy. For instance, a survey of cases conducted by the Holy Office at Saragossa reveals some curious examples of charges which sent some Conversos to prison and others to the stake as relapsed Judaizers. These include the expression of doubts regarding the immaculate conception, the real presence, and the corporate character of the Trinity, as well as a disbelief in Hell, Paradise, or a future life. Careless religious habits were also taken as evidence of Judaism; poor attendance at church, neglect of confession, failure to cross oneself on appropriate occasions, forgetting the words of the *Pater Noster* and the *Ave Maria*, withholding the truth at confession, and eating meat on Friday. In the same category were certain derelictions during the Mass—failure to kneel at the proper moments, eating before Communion, and letting one's attention wander when the Host was raised.

Blasphemies of various kinds appear too. There were jokes about confession and about Christ. One "Judaizer" suggested that the twelve apostles drank too much; another observed that sitting through Mass gave him as much pleasure as a saddle gave to a jackass. And some of the cases involving abuse of the Crucifix have strong overtones of witchcraft. One tiresome case involved the charge of cheating an Old Christian in a business deal.[1]

If the Inquisitors were to avoid wasting time on questionable cases at the cost of neglecting the really serious ones, a more precise definition of Judaism was essential. Early in the 1480's the

---

[1] In later years circumcision became standard evidence of secret Judaizing. In Spain's overseas provinces of the New World, even more wondrous signs were sought. A seventeenth century Inquisitor in New Mexico had a suspected Jew examined for scars of surgery to remove his tail so that he could "pass" into the Christian flock.

Valencia Tribunal issued two documents designed to fill this need. The first, entitled *Audience with a self-confessed Jew*, listed seventeen Jewish practices described by a prisoner. This was followed by the *Declaration of the ceremonies of the Jewish rites given by a certain Jewish rabbi* which said pretty much the same things in greater detail.

However, the most comprehensive "manual" of Jewish customs was the *Censure and Confutation of the Talmud*, which appeared in Segovia about this same time. Prepared under the authority of the local Inquisitors, it was the work of one Antonio de Avila, former Jew and present physician, and friar Alonso Enriquez, also a former Jew and now a Dominican colleague of Torquemada in the latter's cloister at Segovia. It also carried a dedication to Torquemada, written by another friar from the same cloister, Fernando de Santo Domingo. The object of the book, as the authors stated in the introduction, was to place it in the hands of Inquisitor General Torquemada to enable the Inquisition to proceed "with greater confidence against those who [secretly] observe Talmudic rites."

To avoid repetition we have combined these documents into a composite "manual," including in it the most typical examples of Jewish practice which appear over and over in the cases of this period. We have followed closely the language and sense of the originals in an effort to retain their flavor as well as their sentiment.

Manual of Jewish Practices

Preliminary Observations

The Inquisitors must be aware of the ceremonies customarily performed by the Jews so that they can effectively interrogate criminals brought before them and ascertain whether they are confessing the truth about their Judaizing heresies. This manual will also enable the Inquisitors to prompt criminals brought before them to testify fully regarding all the Jewish ceremonies they or their neighbors have secretly practiced. It should also be remembered that the observance of any one of these Jewish practices is sufficient to condemn a professing Christian as a Judaizing apostate from the True Faith. For, as is well known, the Jewish conscience of a Converso can be soothed by observing merely a single one of these rites even if, under the pressure of necessity, the Converso were obliged to neglect all the others. The most common of such rites and ceremonies are those which follow.

The Messiah

They say that the promised Messiah has not yet come but that he will some day come to free them from the captivity they claim they now suffer and to take them to the Promised Land. Thus they deny the Law of Jesus Christ our Redeemer.

Blessing the Children

They pray Jewish prayers and recite the Psalms of David without *gloria patri*. At night they beg forgiveness of one another, the fathers putting their hands on their children's heads, saying: "Of God and of me be blessed." They place the hand on top of the head, dropping it down over the face without crossing themselves. This is done in imitation of the blessing which Jacob gave to his grandchildren Manasseh and Ephraim, the sons of Joseph.

Burying the Fingernails

They cut their nails and bury them in the earth so that no superstitions may be practiced with them and so that they may be collected on the Judgment Day.

Fast Days

On the eve of their Fast days, they wash themselves, cutting their nails and the ends of their hair. They recite Jewish prayers, raising and lowering their heads, their faces turned to the wall. Before they pray they wash their hands with water or rub them with earth, and they dress themselves in white shrouds of twill, tammycloth, or linen, with fringes around the bottom.

Yom Kippur

This Fast day, also known as the day of Atonement, is observed in memory of the forty days that Moses spent on Mount Sinai without eating or drinking, awaiting the light and pardon which God was to give to the people of Israel for the sin of idolatry, which sin God forgave them because of their prayers. And so on Yom Kippur the Jews go barefoot, asking forgiveness of one another, the younger ones kissing the hands of their elders. This Fast day generally falls on the tenth day of the moon in September.[1]

The Feast of Purim

This is in memory of the deliverance of the Jews from Haman, minister of King Ahasuerus of Persia. Ahasuerus liberated the Jews because his life was saved through the efforts of Mordecai, stepfather of Queen Esther, as related in the Book of Esther. The Feast of Purim is preceded the day before by the Fast of Queen Esther, which the Jews also refer to as the "Loss of the holy house."

The Feast of Unleavened Bread

This Feast commemorates the passage of the Jews through the Red Sea. During the seven days it took them to pass through the water they ate nothing but certain cakes [matzohs] which they carried on their shoulders. And therefore the Jews eat only unleavened bread during these seven days in memory of that event, in accordance with the instructions in Exodus: "seven days shall ye eat unleavened bread."

The Feast of Lights

They celebrate the Feast of the small candles, which they light one by one up to ten[2] in number, and afterward they snuff them out again, and they recite Jewish prayers.

---

[1] That is, in the Hebrew calendar, which was (and is) lunar.
[2] Actually nine.

The Feast of Booths

This comes on the fifteenth of September. It is a solemnity which the Jews celebrate in memory of the time when the Israelites left Egypt and wandered forty years in the desert, living in huts made of green boughs, before they entered into the land of Canaan. During this Feast they erect small huts, covering them with willows, fennels and other greens and fruits. These huts must be built exposed to the night air, in a place open to the sky, as was the case with their ancestors in the desert. This Feast lasts nine days, the Jews giving thanks to God because the fruits of the earth have been harvested, and for seven days of the nine they must eat under these shelters.

Feast of the Ram's Horn

This is in memory of the day when God freed Isaac from the sacrifice which his father Abraham was planning for him by substituting for Isaac the ram which Abraham found with its horns caught in the brambles. On this Feast day the Jews blow a horn in memory of that event. This Feast falls on the first day of the new moon in the month of September.

The Jewish Sabbath

They celebrate Saturday as their holy day in honor of the Law of Moses. On that day they put clean linen on the table, clean sheets on the bed, and dress up in clean clothes. They bless the table according to the Jewish custom, and filling a glass with homemade wine, they say certain words over it, after which everyone takes a swallow from it. For this day they also prepare the Sabbath loaf, in memory of the bread which the people of Israel were obligated to give to the high priest of Jerusalem as a sacrifice. In making this Sabbath loaf they throw a small piece of dough into the fire, in accord with the ancient practice of offering a portion of this dough to their high priest. All this is done on

Friday as the Jews do not make fires or perform any other work on Saturday.[1]

Anim

Because the Jews cannot prepare food on Saturday they prepare on Friday a kind of stew called anim. It is made of meat, peas, beans and other vegetables. It is cooked all night Friday and kept hot until mealtime on Saturday. The preparation of this anim on Friday night marks the beginning of the Saturday Sabbath.

Meat

They eat meat and fowl only when it has been killed in the Jewish fashion, which consists of severing its windpipe to drain it completely of blood. For in the Jewish Law they are forbidden to eat any animal which still has blood left in its body. This is why, in Mosaic Law, the Jews are commanded not to eat any animal which has died a natural death, as it is certain to have blood still remaining in its body.

The Sciatic Nerve

They remove the sciatic nerve from the legs of cattle before cooking. This is done in memory of the time when Jacob wrestled with an angel and the angel touched the hollow of Jacob's thigh, putting it out of joint, as it is told in Genesis.

Forbidden Meats

They do not eat pig because Mosaic Law prohibits them from eating animals that do not ruminate. They do not eat rabbit because that same Law forbids them to eat animals that do not have a cloven hoof. And they abstain from eels and fish without scales or fins because Mosaic Law forbids these too.

---

[1] One of the Inquisitors of Seville—a very clever fellow indeed—used to tour the town on Saturday mornings during the winter, inspecting the roofs of the houses to see which chimneys were not smoking. These, of course, would be the chimneys of Conversos who were secretly Judaizing. For they would not light a fire on Saturday nor hire a Christian to do it for fear of being denounced to the Inquisition as Judaizers.

Newborn Children

Their women, after giving birth, do not enter the synagogue for forty days. As soon as the children are born the Jews circumcise them and give them Jewish names. Although they bring them to the True Church to be baptised, under the pretense of being Christians, they wash off the consecrated oil of baptism as soon as they get the children back home. Also, on the seventh night after the birth of a child they fill a basin with water and throw into it gold, silver, a pearl, wheat, barley, and other things. Then they wash the infant in it, reciting certain words which are supposed to preserve the newborn from future dangers.

Ceremony for the Dead

When a Jew is on the point of death they turn his face to the wall in memory of the time when the prophet Isaiah said to King Hezekiah: "Oh king, set thine house in order, for thou shalt die and not live." And then King Hezekiah turned his face to the wall and wept for his sins, and God prolonged his life fifteen more years. And so a Jew about to die turns his face to the wall to weep for his sins. When he dies they wash him with hot water and shave his beard, underarms and other parts of the body. Then they shroud him in new linen with trousers, a clean shirt and a plaited cape. Under his head they place a bag of Palestinian earth and in his mouth a silver coin, pearls or other things. Then they go through his house and pour out the water in his pitchers and water jars. After that they sit on the floor eating fish and olives, but not meat; and finally, they bury the deceased in consecrated Jewish soil.

The Surviving Widow

Jewish Law provides that when a brother dies the surviving brother may marry the widow on the principle of keeping alive the seed of the dead brother. However, if he does not wish to marry his brother's widow he must wear on his right foot a special leather shoe with twelve straps and twelve bows. The widow then comes and spits on him to signify that as the twelve straps of the shoe come untied so too is untied the obligation of either party to marry the other. Each one is then free to marry anyone else. It should also be noted that even if the surviving brother is already married but has no children of his own, he can take his brother's widow as his second wife, for that part of Jewish Law permits a man to take a second wife provided he has no children from the first one. The purpose of this custom of permitting a surviving brother to marry his widowed sister-in-law is to perpetuate the progeny of the deceased. Therefore, the first child born of such a marriage must be named after the dead brother, which is what is meant by the phrase "keeping alive the seed of the dead."

THE ALBORAICO

One other document deserves mention here. As a manual for the detection of secret Judaizers it has none of the practical advantages of those described above. But we may be sure that it was more entertaining reading for the Jew-hating generation of Torquemada.

Moslem tradition tells us that when Mohammed was about to die Allah sent the angel Gabriel to bring him up to Paradise. With him Gabriel brought an animal for the Prophet to ride, called *al-Burak*. It is traditionally represented as a mare with a woman's head and the tail of a peacock, and in the mosque at Jerusalem is an oddly shaped stone said to be the saddle of al-Burak.

In the library at Torquemada's monastery in Segovia was a book called the *Alboraico*, written in 1488 by an anonymous author who clearly loved his work. In this piece of learned nonsense Mohammed's "horse," the Alboraico, becomes the symbolic equivalent of the Judaizing Converso of Spain, and each part of his body represents a particular characteristic of these apostates from the True Faith, as follows:

The Mouth of a Wolf

The Alboraicos of Spain (i.e., the Judaizing Conversos) are

hypocrites and false prophets who call themselves Christians when they are not. They claim the Messiah is yet to come when, as everybody knows, He came over fourteen centuries ago. They say the True Messiah will come in Seville, not as a poor man on an ass but as an emperor, richly attired, riding in a golden chariot and carrying a great sword with which to slay all Christians.

The Face of a Horse

The horse, because of his quickness and daring, is used in war for spilling the blood of humans. Likewise these Alboraicos used their speed and boldness to kill the prophets Isaiah and Zacharias, as well as the apostles and martyrs and our Lord Himself. For they know not the way of peace and the fear of God is not in their eyes. And those who have fled Spain to escape the justice of the Inquisition have, as everybody knows, gone to join the Turks to help spill the blood of Christians.

The Eyes of a Man

They look like human beings but are really devils in disguise.

The Ears of a Dog

As the dog is not ashamed to perform his excretions in public where everybody can see him, so these Alboraicos are not ashamed to perform their heresies and lies and Jewish ceremonies in full view of God. Also, as the dog returns to eat his own vomit, so the Alboraico returns to his Jewish Sabbath and circumcision.

The Neck of a Mare, with a Mane

The mare is useless for any kind of hard work, preferring instead to promenade idly about the square. So too with the Alboraico: he is not any good as a laborer or as a soldier against the enemies of the Faith. Instead, like the mare, he prances about in public in all his finery.

The Body of an Ox

Like the ox he stuffs his belly and thinks only of material

things, priding himself on his palatial home, his expensive furnishings, his wealth and his painted daughters.

The Tail of a Serpent
Like the serpent the Alboraico crawls about on his belly, lying in ambush to spread the poison of his heresies among True Believers.

At the End of the Tail, the Body of a Peacock
This symbolizes his lust for the pomp and vanities of the world as well as his admiration of himself and his own works.

On the Peacock, the Head of a Crane
The crane is a cowardly creature, always in hiding, just as the Alboraico lives in fear and trembling among Christians, always trying to hide his true character from them. It is difficult to kill a crane for he covers himself up with his wings, as the Alboraico protects himself with his great wealth and his winepots.

One Foreleg: the Leg of a Man Clothed in Fancy Hose and with a Shoe on the Foot
This symbolizes his great pride, his love of luxury and his madness in wishing to subjugate Christians.

The other Foreleg: the Leg of a Horse with a Horseshoe
Whenever they get a Christian in their power they kick and squeeze and crush him like grapes in a winepress.

One Hindleg: the Leg of an Eagle with Claws Extended
They live by rapine, robbing the churches, buying bishoprics, canonries and other Church offices, taking holy orders and despoiling good Christians, all the while believing nothing of the Faith or the Christian ceremonies they perform. They also cheat the workers and the poor and rob from widows and orphans.

The other Hindleg: the Leg of a Lion without its Claws
They descend from Judas, who is compared to a lion. But they are without strength, like a lion without his claws. They will never become strong until they accept Jesus Christ.

The Hair of all Colors

They perform all kinds of evil. Among Jews they say they are Jews; among Christians they claim to be Christians. They adapt themselves readily to whatever pretense they think will do them the most good.

It Eats Anything and Everything

They eat the same meats as Christians and Moors; they eat Jewish foods also. They even eat during both the Christian and Jewish Fast days.

It Is Neither Male nor Female

They are sodomists. The tribe of Benjamin sinned in sodomy and on one day 125,000 of them—men, women and children—died because of it. From the Jews the practice of sodomy passed to the Moors, who passed it on to the Alboraicos of Spain.

A Richly Adorned Saddle

They lust after wealth and the material things of this world, caring nothing for the riches of the spirit.

The Saddle Made of the Wood of the Fig Tree

Their synagogue is like the fig tree which Christ cursed, after which it dried up and never again bore fruit. Likewise their synagogue has never borne fruit for Paradise, since none of its members will be saved.

The Stirrups Made of Many Metals

The Alboraico has many origins. Some were Jews converted by Christ, after which they turned against and rejected Him. Saint Peter and the other Apostles converted some, but they too returned to the synagogue. In our own times many others were converted to the True Faith and have since relapsed into Judaism. Also, in their many captivities and wanderings they have married with women of other races and are now mixed breeds of many metals. In addition they have adhered to many and diverse heresies throughout their history, including the errors of the Sadducees and Pharisees among others.

The Bridle of Fire and a Sword for the Reins

If the Alboraico is not held in strong check he will spread the fire of heresy from one end of Spain to the other and will ultimately destroy the whole of these Christian realms.

Throughout this little study our unknown author buttresses his tortured allegories with appropriate passages wrenched from Scripture. He also seasons his work with secular tidbits from the human gutters of hatred. We are told, for example, that the backsliding Converso is pompous, vainglorious, wicked, cruel, impenitent, inhuman, insane, damned, condemned, scorned of God. He is consumed with indolence, wanton arrogance and diabolical envy. He is an unbeliever, a deceiver, heretic, evil-doer, traitor, false prophet, liar, idolater, hypocrite, a wolf in sheep's clothing. He comes from a foul lineage and a cursed generation of thieves, plunderers and blasphemers. He is a devil, dog-man, mongrel, sodomite, venomous viper, poisonous asp. His temple is the synagogue of Satan and he is the Antichrist on earth.

Thus the Alboraico, a ballad of hate in a chorus of death and destruction, transformed by the alchemy of righteousness into a hymn of exaltation to Almighty God.

CHAPTER 9

Denunciation for Survival

SOON AFTER TORQUEMADA ESTABLISHED A TRIBUNAL of the Holy Office in Toledo, a resident Converso appeared before the newly appointed Inquisitors to make a voluntary confession of his many sins.

> *I, Juan Alvarez of Seville,* (he began) *silk worker and resident of this city of Toledo in the parish of San Roman, kiss the sacred hands of Your Reverend Lordships and present myself before you with the greatest contrition and grief of soul, to confess and make manifest my guilt and the sins which I have committed against our Lord and Redeemer Jesus Christ, and against His Holy Faith.*

Twenty-five years before, when Juan Alvarez was a mere boy, his father sent him to Seville as an apprentice to a Jewish silversmith named Mayr Abenbilla. The latter not only initiated young Juan into the mysteries of silversmithing but also into all the ceremonies of the Law of Moses. Since he was so young and plastic, Juan Alvarez soon was convinced that he could never be saved outside the Mosaic Law and although still nominally a Christian he began to live like a Jew. After three years of this he became an apprentice to a milliner in Seville. The latter, who posed in public as a Christian, practiced Judaism in secret and encouraged Juan—who, of course, needed no encouraging—to continue in his evil ways. From Seville he moved on to Cordova where he lived for a time with another Converso and his wife, all three of them happily practicing Judaism while passing as Christians.

Five years ago Juan returned to Toledo where he was happy to discover that the city was full of Conversos living as Jews behind closed doors. These included his father, mother and four brothers, their friends and neighbors, as well as Juan's various employers, fellow-workers and all of their friends and neighbors. He was soon caught up in a round of Passover celebrations, Jewish prayer meetings, wakes for the dead, Hebrew dietary delights of food and wine, and all the other paraphernalia by which wicked Conversos testify to their attachment to the Law of Moses.

He finally settled down in a house of his own, with a Converso girl who had two young children by a husband who was permanently out of town. Together the new lovers ate unleavened bread, took ceremonial baths, cut the fat from meat, burned candles on Friday night, put on clean clothes for Saturday, fasted on Jewish Fast Days, eschewed Christian meats and fish without scales, celebrated Lent by elaborately ignoring it, attended Jewish Wakes, entertained their backsliding Converso friends, ran an underground railroad for fugitives from the Inquisition, and raised their children to be bad Christians.

By the time he finished his confession, Juan Alvarez had denounced all his friends, employers, co-workers and neighbors, in addition to his common-law wife, his two stepchildren, his mother, father, and all his brothers. He did this, he said, because he had now seen the Christian light. He grieved for his sins. His heart was filled with repentance. He wanted only to be clasped to the bosom of the True Faith, reposing in bliss in the outstretched arms of the Redeemer.

Juan Alvarez had come forth voluntarily under the Edict of Grace, which promised Inquisitorial mercy to all Conversos who purged themselves without prompting. This was an operational procedure established by Torquemada early in the Inquisitorial game. By promising mercy to those who told all, it traded on the common human fears which guarantee success to organized persecution everywhere. Soon after his elevation as Inquisitor General, Torquemada outlined elaborate instructions designed to facilitate the apprehension of derelict Christians. Wherever a new tribunal was established, the Inquisitors were to publish an Edict of Grace, allowing an interval of thirty to forty days,

> *so that all persons, both men and women, who find themselves guilty of any sin or heresy or apostasy, or of practicing or observing the rites or ceremonies of the Jews, or of any others whatsoever, which are contrary to the Christian religion, may come forward and make manifest and confess their errors in full, and further confess all they know and remember about the said crime regarding both themselves and other persons who may have fallen into the said error.*

Those who cooperated, Torquemada promised, would be exempted from the penalties of death, life imprisonment, and full property confiscation usually reserved for the obstinate. They could expect instead a charitable reception and some kind of fine, as well as a penance for therapeutic purposes, in keeping with the wish of their Catholic Majesties, Ferdinand and Isabella, to extend clemency to all those who sincerely hungered for reconciliation to the True Faith.

Included in Torquemada's instructions, however, was a warning to anyone who thought he could cheat justice by making any old kind of confession. He had to tell all he knew, not only about himself but about everybody else, including members of his own family down to minor children. If it was later discovered that a penitent sinner had held back any information, his reconciliation to the Faith was automatically invalid and he was to be dealt with as an impenitent heretic, i.e., eminently eligible for roasting. Those heretics, of course, who failed to take advantage of the Edict of Grace, were ineligible for any of its benefits and were to be regarded as contumacious deceivers to be prosecuted with full Inquisitorial rigor.

As an economical method of collecting evidence against heretics, the Edict of Grace left little to be desired. Upwards of a thousand people came forward and confessed at Valencia. In Toledo the number approached three thousand, and the tribunals in smaller towns counted them in the hundreds—all within the brief period of thirty to forty days. However, as a method of preserving human dignity, the Edict of Grace left everything to be desired. Self-confessed Judaizers raked over their past lives, baring every shabby detail they could think of, grovelling and degrading themselves in their anxiety to impress the Inquisitors with their sincerity. In addition to self-denunciation, they wallowed in orgies of accusation against others. Servants denounced their masters; the poor denounced the rich; husbands and wives, sweethearts and lovers denounced each other; friends denounced friends; neighbors denounced neighbors; parents denounced their children and children denounced their parents.

The case of one Brianda de Bardaxi will serve as one of many such examples of these dismal exercises in fear and hatred. Brianda, a Converso of Saragossa, was on bad terms with her mother Salvadora, who thought Brianda had received too large a share of the family property. Mother Salvadora was supported in this opinion by her daughter-in-law, an elderly widow named Aldonza, who felt that she also had been short-changed for the benefit of Brianda. Between the two of them these disgruntled ladies managed to nag Brianda to desperate measures. When the Inquisition came to Saragossa, Brianda hurried over to announce that when she was five years old, she had seen her mother and sister-in-law fast on a Jewish holiday.

Mother Salvadora and sister Aldonza were immediately jailed. They had no doubts about who had put them there; they confessed to observing some Jewish Fast days, and swore that Brianda had taken part in them also. Meanwhile, more of Brianda's enemies were adding to her troubles. A former neighbor, with whom

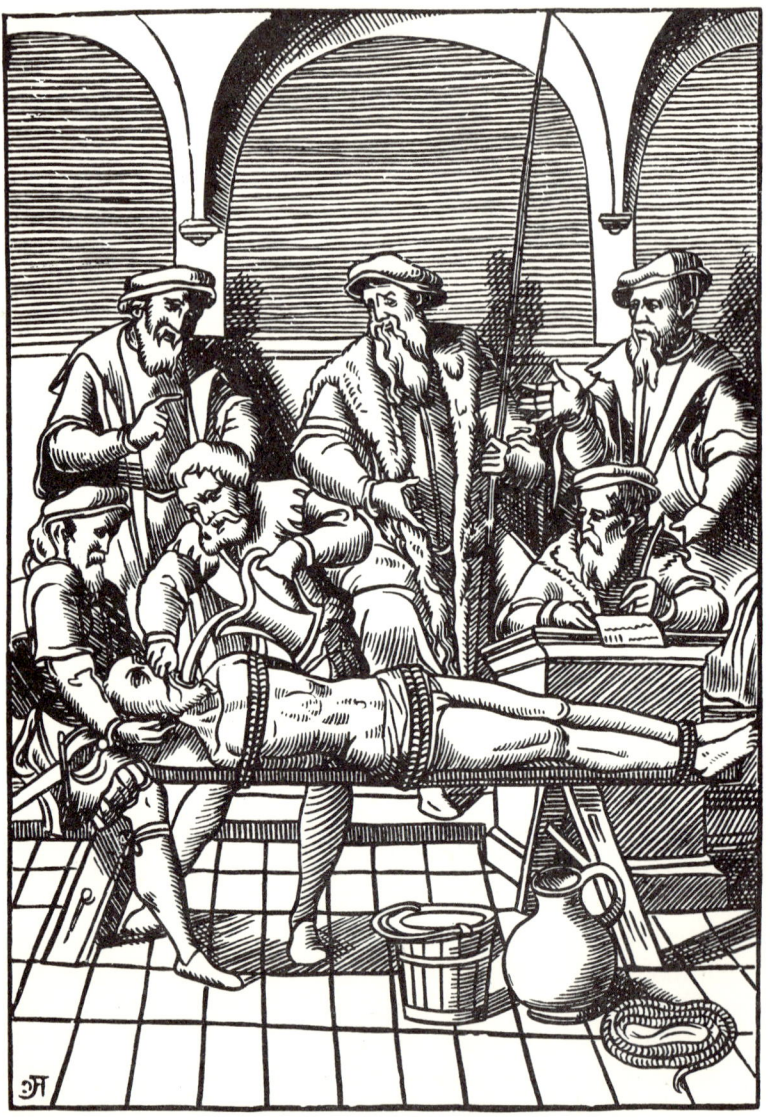

THE WATER TORTURE. (From a 16th century woodcut.)

Brianda had been feuding for some years, had been seized by the Holy Office as a Judaizer. In his confession he claimed that Brianda was also secretly a Jew, and was supported in his accusation by his wife and two daughters, who didn't like Brianda either.

Proceedings were immediately begun against Brianda, who was obviously made of sterner stuff than her accusers. All the Inquisitors could get out of her, under repeated questioning, was the admission that when she was about five years old she had taken an occasional bite of unleavened bread. Except for that one childhood indiscretion, she insisted, she had never been other than a good Christian. She also presented a parade of witnesses who testified to the bad blood between Brianda and her accusers, and swore to her exceptionally fervent Christian character: she lived like a nun; she prayed at least an hour every day; she often wore a hairshirt, and she ate fat and lard with obvious gusto.

Clearly, somebody was lying. Torquemada's men, like their chief, automatically assumed that it was the accused. So the Inquisitors of Saragossa resorted to that sure solvent of all doubts —the machinery of torture. Brianda was spread-eagled on a trestle, her head lower than her feet, her arms and legs tightly bound with cords. The cords were then twisted with a winch, cutting deep corrugations in the flesh and producing the most intense agony. When Brianda still gasped out her innocence, the water torture was added to encourage her to tell the truth. While she was still bound to the trestle, her nostrils were plugged and a stream of water was poured down her throat, stopping just short of complete strangulation. After an hour and a half of this, Brianda cracked and blurted out a tolerably ample confession to the effect that she had been a secret Judaizer for years. Three days later she revoked her confession, asserting that it was all a lie extracted by torture. So back to the torture chamber she went, but just as her treatment was about to start, Brianda fainted dead away. Unable to revive her, the frustrated Inquisitors had her carried back to her cell.

After four years in an Inquisition dungeon, with torture for diversion, the only firm cooperation the Inquisitors were able to get from Brianda was the admission that she had nibbled unleavened bread at the age of five. She was therefore pronounced to be "vehemently suspect" of Judaizing, was forced to abjure her heresies in a public Auto de Fe, and to pay a fine consisting of one third of all her property. Since the modern apologists for the Inquisition assure us that it was not really as bad as the "prejudiced" historians say it was, we like to think that some good came out of the trial of Brianda de Bardaxi. Perhaps the Inquisition, by appropriating a sizable chunk of Brianda's property, restored harmony in the family hitherto rent by inequalities in the distribution of wealth which had now been leveled out by the Holy Office.

In his instructions regarding the Edict of Grace, Torquemada was careful to provide for the reopening of a case against any reconciled person whose confession was later discovered to be unsatisfactory. The circumstances under which such action could be taken were described by Torquemada in these words:

> *If some person or persons among those who come forward do not confess the ENTIRE truth regarding everything they know about themselves or about others in connection with the crime of heresy, ESPECIALLY IN SERIOUS AND OUTSTANDING MATTERS AND CRIMES, it is presumed that they gained reconciliation through deception.*

The proper application of these instructions might vex the ingenuity of a Solomon. In Torquemada's day they were often no more than an excuse to stoke the fires. There are numerous instances of self-confessed penitents who, after having been reconciled, were later retried and then burned at the stake on the ground that they had deliberately withheld important information from the Inquisitors. In some cases the charge was very likely justified, but in a great many others the Inquisitors tempered justice with no quarter. Two examples, from among the many cases of this kind, illustrate the pattern.

When the Edict of Grace was proclaimed in Ciudad Real, a

great many of the town's residents came forward to denounce either themselves or their friends, or both. So prolific were these revelations that in the two short years of its existence—before its transfer to the larger metropolitan center of Toledo—the tribunal at Ciudad Real burned almost three hundred Judaizers, in person or in effigy (depending on which was available), and reconciled some two hundred more.

Among the earliest arrivals at Inquisition headquarters was one Maria Pampano, with a tale about a husband who was a heretic and a brute. When she married Juan Pampano twenty-five years before, he was a perfectly good Christian. But after they had been married for about nine years, her husband suddenly announced that henceforth he intended to live like a Jew and he expected Maria to do likewise. However, Maria refused, for she had been raised as a good Christian and never entertained the terrible thought of being anything else. But husband Juan was determined, and life in the Pampano household turned into a prolonged reign of terror. He forced Maria to live like a Jew and he beat her unmercifully when she protested. After six years of this, to Maria's relief, husband Juan left her and dropped out of sight. About four years later he turned up on her doorstep, begging her to come away with him. She refused even to let him in the house, so he went away and she never saw him again. Now she wished to confess her sins of many years ago and to state that, under violent pressure from her husband, she had (1) refrained from working on Saturdays, (2) prepared Saturday's food on Friday, (3) eaten this food on Saturday, (4) eaten meat prepared Jewish style, and (5) baked unleavened bread and eaten it. Also, Maria confessed, after her husband had left her, she had through force of habit continued "for a while" to observe the Jewish Sabbath. She soon came to her senses, however, confessed her sin to a priest, and for the last nine or ten years had always lived like a good Christian.

This confession seemed honest enough, so Maria Pampano was forgiven by the Inquisitors and formally reconciled to the True

Faith. Two months later, to her astonishment and horror, she was in jail and on trial for her life as an impenitent heretic. It seems that some of her neighbors had also made confessions under the Edict of Grace. Several of them had, among a great many other things, confirmed the accusations which Maria had already made against herself. However, a former servant in the Pampano household, who had a sharp eye for unorthodox details, enumerated a number of examples of Maria's Judaizing habits which the latter had not specifically itemized in her own confession.

Maria was now formally charged with making a fraudulent confession and with being a stealthy dissembler and obstinate heretic with a heart hardened against the True Faith. The Inquisition prosecutor therefore asked that she be relaxed for burning on the ground that she had not included in her confession the following admissions:

(1) She refrained from working on Saturdays.
(2) She gave the Jewish ceremonial bath to her newborn children.
(3) She indoctrinated her children in the Law of Moses.
(4) She ate chicken during Lent.
(5) She participated in Jewish prayer sessions at home.
(6) She observed the Jewish Passover.

Maria pointed out—correctly—that she had already confessed to the first charge. The second, third and fourth charges she flatly denied. As for the last two, she protested that they were implicit in her own confession that she had been forced by her husband to observe many Jewish customs. If she failed to specify every last detail, she begged the Inquisitors to consider that her crimes covered a period of ten to twenty years before, and that she was bound to forget some things.

To substantiate her claims of innocence, Maria called on some of her neighbors as character witnesses. They proved to be a sorry lot: three of them had known Maria only a few years, and although they said nice things about her, the Inquisitors were only interested in her activities long before then. The other two witnesses met the time requirement, but they were obviously so frightened in the face of the dreaded Inquisition that their testimony did Maria as much harm as good. The first one, a neighbor lady, when asked by the Inquisitors if Maria observed the Lenten season, replied with excruciating caution. She remembered, she said, that once or twice in the thirty years she had known Maria, the latter had borrowed a head covering from her because, so she had said, she wanted to take her daughter to confession. However, this witness hastened to add that she never actually saw Maria's daughter at confession. Then, when the Inquisitors wanted to know whether the witness had ever seen Maria observe the Jewish Sabbath, she said she did not know, although there were times when she felt "slightly suspicious" about that matter.

The other witness was Maria's godson. All he would say was that he had seen seen his godmother go to church to hear mass, and ignore the Jewish Sabbath by working. But when the Inquisitors asked him about the other charges against her, Maria's godson, although he had known her intimately all his life, could only repeat over and over that he knew nothing about anything that ever went on inside his godmother's house.

The Inquisitors were satisfied that Maria Pampano was guilty as charged. In a public Auto de Fe early in 1484 she was formally declared to be a deceiver, dissembler, false penitent, secret Judaizer, heretic and apostate, and was burned to ashes.

At almost the same time that Maria Pampano was getting married to the man whose religious idiosyncrasies were to bring her to the stake, a young widow named Beatriz Nuñez was leaving Ciudad Real to seek her marital fortunes in nearby Guadalupe. Beatriz had been born and raised in Ciudad Real in a family of secret Judaizers. There she had married a Converso of similar habits and raised a small family of two sons, both of whom Beatriz and her husband indoctrinated in the Mosaic mysteries.

When her first husband died in 1465, Beatriz moved to Guadalupe where she married again and began raising a second family. There was, at that time, no Spanish Inquisition; Torquemada was still savoring his dreams of purification in the cloister at Segovia. However, in 1465 there was a brief flareup of persecution under Henry IV of Castile, urged on by Alonso de Espina and some of his clerical colleagues. Beatriz Nuñez had hardly settled down in Guadalupe with her new husband when he was seized by the local authorities as a secret Judaizer and after some time in prison was given a stiff fine and admonished to mend his ways.

Some eighteen years later, when the Inquisition set about purging Ciudad Real, a number of Beatriz' hometown friends and relatives, including her first husband and one of her sons, were burned—the quick in person and the dead in effigy.

If Beatriz had any hopes of escaping the Inquisition by remaining in Guadalupe, such hopes were quickly dashed. A little over a year after the tribunal opened at Ciudad Real, another one was established in Guadalupe. If the one at Ciudad Real was rigorous, the branch at Guadalupe was ferocious. Doctor Francisco Sanchez was sent over from Ciudad Real to lend his experience to efficient operations at Guadalupe. He was placed under the authority of the prior of the local Geronomite monastery, friar Nuño de Arevalo, whose determination to cauterize the sores of Judaism more than compensated for his lack of experience. In the few short months of its operation, before the Guadalupe tribunal was absorbed by its big brother in Toledo, seven Autos de Fe were held in the macabre setting of the cemetery in front of friar Nuño's monastery. In all, fifty-three men and women were burned alive, including a monk from friar Nuño's own cloister. Forty-six corpses were dug up and burned. The effigies of twenty-five fugitives were consigned to the flames. Sixteen sinners were jailed for life, and "innumerable others," the early accounts tell us, were condemned to perpetual exile and confiscation of all property. Not one single person was reconciled to the Faith. So pleased was our Lady with the good work that Her image at Guadalupe began spewing forth miracles in such prodigious quantities that

Inquisitor Sanchez, trying to record them for posterity, broke down from writer's cramp.

Into this den of virtue came a frightened Beatriz Nuñez in January, 1485, seeking the mercy promised under the Edict of Grace. She confessed at length about her earlier Judaizing years in Ciudad Real, listing many specific details and adding that she had practiced "all the other ceremonies" of Judaism. In Guadalupe, she went on, her new husband's heretical misfortunes had made her much more cautious. Here she practiced Judaism in secret to avoid her husband's frightened anger, the servants' prying eyes, and embarrassing questions from her children. Even so, she managed a few Judaizing accomplishments: she avoided pork and fish without scales, she removed the fat from meat, she begged off housework on Saturdays, and even observed "several" Jewish Fast days. Furthermore, Beatriz freely admitted, she would have lived like a full-time Jewess if she hadn't been afraid of being found out. Now, however, she saw the error of her heretical ways and repented of her sins, begging forgiveness and seeking reconciliation under the terms of the Edict of Grace. Beatriz then concluded with the following pathetic plea to her judges:

> *And because my memory is poor and it is possible that I have erred in other things which I do not at the moment recall over such a long period of time or because I am so upset, I protest before your Lordships that if I should remember anything else, I will immediately come forward to declare it and to ask penance for it. And to cleanse myself further I hereby state that if any persons have or shall come forth to declare anything against me in addition to what I have already confessed, and if they are persons in whom your Lordships have confidence, then I confess beforehand that whatever they may say is true and I ask penance for it, submitting myself at all times to the correction of the Holy Mother Church.*

Even friar Nuño was satisfied, at least for the moment, with this confession, and Beatriz Nuñez was formally reconciled to the True Faith and set free. A few weeks later she was picked up on orders of friar Nuño and imprisoned for trial as a false penitent and deceiver of the Holy Office.

Beatriz had obviously been deluding herself with the notion that she had concealed her evil secrets from the help. Seven garrulous maids from the Nuñez household—champions of the Faith all—came forward to contribute heretical scraps for the new case against their mistress. These were carefully pieced together by the Inquisition prosecutor into a formal accusation demanding that Beatriz Nuñez be burned at the stake on the ground that she had omitted the following details from her voluntary confession:

(1) She bathed during her period.[1]
(2) She participated in Jewish funeral rites.
(3) She blessed her children without crossing herself.
(4) She indoctrinated her children in Judaism, and washed off the oil of their Christian baptism.
(5) She ate meat only when prepared in the Jewish fashion.
(6) She confessed that in Ciudad Real she used to light candles on Friday nights, remove the sciatic nerve from the leg of meat, and prepare Saturday's meal on Friday. She did not, however, confess that she had also done these things in Guadalupe.

The substance of Beatriz' defense appears sound enough. She pointed out that she had already confessed to observing all the Jewish practices she thought she could hide, and to a desire to follow them all. She had also admitted that her faulty memory and personal agitation undoubtedly made her leave out some details about her errors of the past twenty years, and she had even confessed beforehand to the truth of any future denunciations which might include specific details she had forgotten herself. It was on this basis, Beatriz reminded her captors, that she had been forgiven and reconciled to the Faith by the Inquisitors themselves.

---

[1] Although this was not a Jewish religious custom, it apparently was a practice abhorred by orthodox Christians.

Even the zealous friar Nuño was sensitive to the legal niceties of this case. If Beatriz were to be burned—a foregone conclusion—it would have to be done according to the rules. And the rules required that she make a specific confession that she had deliberately withheld important information in her original confession. Fortunately the machinery of torture was always available to solve such knotty problems as these. Beatriz was therefore stretched out on the rack where, with the help of the Inquisitors, she blurted out a suitably incriminating confession and once more begged mercy for her sins. This time, however, her plea was denied. For, as the prosecutor pointed out, she had confessed her misdeeds only when no other course was open to her. Therefore, it was clear that she was not truly contrite or repentant. Therefore, it was equally clear that she was an impenitent heretic. Therefore, she should be burned at the stake. Therefore, Beatriz Nuñez was burned at the stake July 23, 1485.

CHAPTER 10

The Remnant

WHEN THE NEWS ARRIVED IN TOLEDO in 1485 that a tribunal of the Holy Office was about to be established there, a number of Conversos sought safety elsewhere. A band of six such culprits made their way to the port of Valencia where they bought a small boat and set sail for a foreign port. A few days later Providence stirred up capricious winds which blew them back to Valencia. They were immediately seized and sent back to Toledo where they became the first burning victims of the Inquisition in that city.

Flight from Spain was becoming a common Converso occupation, and Torquemada worked hard to seal off the borders. He even secured the cooperation of the Pope, who used his spiritual powers to persuade foreign potentates to return Inquisition fugitives to Spanish justice. Even so, the number of escapees grew yearly, and fortunately for civilization they included the maternal ancestors of Montaigne, who emigrated to France after one of the clan was burned at Saragossa.

If he could not destroy the bodies of those who escaped him, Torquemada could still ravish their memory and visit their sins on subsequent generations. Escaped persons were formally tried in absentia, solemnly condemned at the Auto de Fe, and as solemnly burned in effigy. Their guilt was distributed among their heirs in the form of infamous memory and dishonor, as well as proscription from public office in church or state.

The same penalties were visited on those who died before their heresy was detected. In his Instructions to the various tribunals, Torquemada directed that if a deceased party were found guilty, his property was to be confiscated and his name erased from the roll of the righteous by digging up his bones and burning them at the Auto de Fe. This rule applied to anybody who had died within the last fifty years, although the enthusiasm of local Inquisitors on one occasion prompted them to burn a heretical corpse which had been blaspheming holy burial ground for a good seventy years. Some kind of record for brevity was made in another case when a Converso cadaver was summoned for trial in Toledo almost before rigor mortis had set in. One Fernando Alfonso, who had apparently lived as a good Christian all his life, was heard to mumble a Jewish prayer just before he expired. He was immediately denounced and a case was formally opened against him. We do not know the result, since his trial record is not complete. In any case, Fernando was probably beyond caring, although the outcome meant a great deal to his heirs who stood to lose their inheritance to the Inquisition.

The burning of effigies and bones probably compensated somewhat for the absence of live originals. But in the very heart of the Christian community there lived a body of unbelievers whom the Inquisition could not touch unless they made an overt assault on Christianity. The Inquisition, as a domestic arm of the Christian church, had authority to deal only with crimes of heresy within that church. The Jew, by definition, was beyond its jurisdiction. Though he rejected the Redeemer, lived in infidelity, and blasphemed the True Faith by his mere existence, yet he was immune from punishment so long as he continued, with his stiff-necked pertinacity, to live under the Law of Moses in preference to the Truth of Christ.

There were ways, of course, of making a Jew eligible for Inquisitorial attention by encouraging him to accept Christian baptism. We have already seen this technique in operation under the initial guiding spirit of Archdeacon Ferdinand Martinez in 1391. By the mid-fifteenth century the main interest of the orthodox had shifted to the growing Converso element as a Frankenstein of subversion among the Faithful. There was always time, however, to make life miserable for the Jews. They were banished from Barcelona in 1425, although the edict was not rigidly enforced. In 1450, the Jewish remnant of Seville begged the protection of King John II against the preachings of a Franciscan friar who was exhorting the local populace to smite the Jews of Seville as their fathers had done sixty years before. A few years later John's successor, Henry IV, sent a royal order throughout Castile. "Prelates, powerful men, clergy, and common people," he lamented, were raising up violence against the Jews to "take by force their synagogues, burial grounds and property and to do other bad things to them." Henry expressed the royal displeasure over such attacks as a threat to an important source of kingly revenue.

There were also some Ritual Murders, of course. Friar Alonso de Espina records several in the 1450's, and in 1468 Torquemada witnessed the punishment of a band of Hebrew assassins in Segovia. They were accused of crucifying a Christian boy at Sepulveda, a small town near Segovia, with the customary dismal consequences of drawing and quartering, hanging, and burning.

Ferdinand and Isabella were as determined to keep the Jews in their place as they were to purge the Conversos. Their employment of Jewish advisers like Don Abraham Seneor had no bearing where the defense of the True Faith was concerned. The destructive Ordinances of 1412, which had been neglected for some years, were re-enacted under the Catholic Monarchs and vigorously enforced. Also revived in full force were the edicts expelling all Jews from Barcelona, the rigid segregation laws, and the prohibition against the employment of Jewish physicians. Where the clerical and royal health were at stake, the latter prohibition did not apply. Torquemada's Dominicans obtained special permission from the Pope to employ Jewish physicians on the plea that there were few doctors of the True Faith in Spain. The Catholic Kings also employed a Jewish physician and, if we can trust the word of contemporaries, it almost cost them the life of their son Prince Juan. It seems the prince was much taken with a golden ball which the royal physician (Maestre Ribas Altas) wore about his neck. After a good deal of boyish wheedling and nagging he finally persuaded the reluctant doctor to give it to him. He soon discovered how to pry the locket open and, to his horror, found inside an obscene miniature of the Savior saluting the royal physician's rump. Prince Juan was so distressed that he fell ill and began wasting away. His distraught father finally coaxed the secret from him and burned the Jew alive, after which the prince immediately began to mend.

The People were happy to follow the royal lead against the Jews. A Franciscan friar excited riots in Jerez with strenuous denunciations of the Jews there as sodomites as well as Antichrists. The duke of Alva burned a rabbi and some of his flock accused of throwing stones at a Cross on Good Friday. The city fathers of Cuenca banned all Jews from town, except for physicians, who were permitted to visit the city as long as was necessary to cure Christian ailments. In Avila the local citizens decided to enforce personally the laws requiring Jews to wear only the plainest clothing. They invaded the ghetto and broke into Jewish homes, plundering them of jewelry, silk clothing, and any fancy trimmings which caught their eye. They mauled the Jewish women, beat up their protesting husbands and wrecked their homes, in the ancient tradition of hooliganism parading under Virtue's banners.

The Crown was not amused. Persecution of Jews must be guided by statutory regulations, not by popular whimsy. The Jews were an important source of revenue for the holy war against the Moors stubbornly holding out in the southern corner of Andalusia. Ferdinand and Isabella threatened stern punishment for assaults on the Jewish community, and in 1485 they addressed a strongly worded proclamation to all citizens of the realm commanding them to pay their just debts to their Jewish creditors in the interests of the financial solvency of the Crown. This was followed by orders to the municipal authorities of Burgos and Bilbao revoking their punitive financial laws against the Jewish communities there.

Jewish agents on missions for the Crown had to be protected beforehand from the general populace. We can appreciate how hazardous it was for a Jew to travel around Spain from the provisions of a blanket edict issued in 1488 on behalf of the Jew Samuel Abolafia. Every person in every city, town, or place through which the royal Jew passed, was warned not to molest him in any way. No money was to be extorted from him under any pretext whatever. He was not to be abused, or mistreated, imprisoned, or killed, for he was under the royal protection.

We get an occasional glimpse of the tense struggle at court between Torquemada and Don Abraham Seneor, who used all his influence with Ferdinand and Isabella to save his fellow Jews from the destruction Torquemada was planning for them. The two antagonists had supported the union of the Catholic Kings, each in accordance with his own expectations of what it might mean for Spanish Judaism. Don Abraham undoubtedly had something to do with the Crown's apparent reluctance to allow their subjects a free hand against the Jews. On one occasion he was personally instrumental in thwarting such action by one of Torquemada's disciples in the monastery of Segovia. Friar Antonio de la Peña undertook a popular preaching campaign against the Jews. He wept copiously, and his audience wept with him, over the wicked ways of the sons of Moses, and he demanded that the Faithful burn down the ghetto and destroy the "wolves" within. The Jews of Segovia complained to Don Abraham who interceded with the Crown, and Torquemada's Dominican cohort was effectively silenced by royal order.

But time and circumstances were on the side of the Inquisitor General, and the best Don Abraham could hope for was a delaying action. Although Jews were normally beyond the Inquisition's reach, they could be brought to trial for subversive activities against the True Faith. Under this provision Torquemada used the machinery of orthodoxy to build a case against the Jews in general as a threat to the security of Christianity in Spain. With evidence of a Jewish conspiracy to subvert the Church and, by implication, the State itself, he would be in a strong position to bring about the final destruction of Judaism in the Spanish peninsula.

The Jews performed a double function for the Inquisition. They were employed as informants against backsliding Conversos. Many Jews undoubtedly looked on this with repugnance, so Torquemada forced the Spanish rabbis to demand it under pain of excommunication from the synagogue. Some Jews, however, apparently got a vengeful pleasure out of compromising their former co-religionists. In some of the extant trials of this period, the accusations of Jewish witnesses are too patently absurd and contradictory to be taken seriously. In one trial a Jewish informant admitted that he had given much testimony against Conversos "regarding things he knew about as well as things he did not know about." And at Toledo in 1488 eight Jews were torn with hot pincers and stoned to death for giving false testimony against Conversos. It was not for moral turpitude that they were so savagely executed, but for their "attempts to discredit the Holy Office," as the record blandly tells us.

Torquemada's "evidence" of a Jewish conspiracy to undermine Church and State is hardly impressive on the basis of any intrinsic judgment. But to people who are already persuaded of the truth of a proposition, the flimsiest "evidence" constitutes positive proof. In fact, even the lack of evidence proves only that the Enemy is diabolically clever at covering his tracks. As proof of his claims, Torquemada was able to lay before the Crown some choice material from Inquisition cases involving Jewish aggressions against the Faith. Extensive investigations of the ghetto at Huesca revealed that Christians were being seduced into Judaism by the local rabbis who were performing secret circumcisions during the late night hours. Equally shocking was the disclosure that a rabbi of Huesca was kidnapped and imprisoned by his peers in order to prevent him from carrying out his intention to convert to Christianity. In Guadalupe the Inquisitors turned up a Jew who had been living (unbaptized) for forty years as a friar in the local Geronomite monastery. He was promptly burned in front of the monastery gates, but there was a widespread suspicion that others like him were poisoning the religious orders all over Spain. Other trials revealed political as well as religious treason among the Jews. It was reported that they not only believed that the Messiah was yet to come, but that he would arrive very soon in the person of the Sultan of Turkey. As they had welcomed the Moors in the eighth century, the Jews were looking forward to the Sultan's conquest of Spain. The Sultan, they claimed, was the defender of Mosaic Law and the destroyer of Christian Law, and would come as Jehovah's instrument to slay the Christians and free the Jews from bondage.

Combining such evidence with the zeal that convinces, Torquemada achieved some modest results. Ferdinand and Isabella expelled the Jews from half a dozen major cities in a series of edicts whose language was clearly inspired by the Inquisitor General. The royal order banishing the Jews from Saragossa in 1486, for example, might well have been written by Torquemada himself.

> *It appears from experience* (announced the king) *that the damaging inroads of heresy among Christians have resulted from communication between Jews and New Christians. The only effective remedy, therefore, is to remove these Jews from among New Christians, as we have already done in the archbishopric of Seville and the bishoprics of Cordova and Jaen. Now, in view of the harm done by the Jews of Saragossa, it is our will that the Jews of that city also be expelled from both the city and the entire archbishopric as well as from the bishopric of Santa Maria. A formal order for said ex-*

pulsion will accordingly be prepared by the devout Father (Torquemada), *prior of the monastery of Santa Cruz.*

This was a step in the right direction toward Torquemada's goal of complete expulsion. Ferdinand and Isabella, however, were not yet willing to commit themselves to such a drastic step. There were, of course, potent considerations in favor of it. Isabella's celebrated piety was the kind which impels a certain type of True Believer to destroy those who worship false gods, and she very likely shared her confessor's convictions about a Jewish conspiracy against the Faith. By this time too the political confusions of the past seven centuries had been focussed into a Great Crusade about to be consummated by glorious victory. The last of the Moorish kings in Spain was at bay behind the walls of Granada, and his days were clearly numbered. Spain's mission was now revealed: unification under the sword and the Cross; exile or death to unbelievers. On a more secular level, the Catholic Kings would be relieved of the anxieties of disaffection among the masses who persisted in taking the law into their own hands where Jews were concerned, despite the sternest admonitions from the throne. Expulsion of the Jews would unquestionably be a popular action, and even the most powerful despot does well to keep an ear cocked to the rumblings of the masses.

But then, the Jews had been on the Spanish scene as long as the Christians themselves. They were a capable, hardworking people who had serviced the royal machinery with money and brains, and even now continued to do so. Could the Crown do as well without them as it did with them? Except for Jews like Abraham Seneor, who were profitably employed in the royal service, the vast majority of Moses' children were safely locked up in the ghetto where they could not brainwash Christians. Perhaps the status quo could be maintained indefinitely.

Torquemada pressed his case. Abraham Seneor pleaded for his kinsmen.

The Crown hesitated.

It was time for a Ritual Murder.

CHAPTER 11

The Ritual Murder of La Guardia

EARLY IN JUNE, 1490, a Converso by the name of Benito Garcia was returning to his home in La Guardia from a pilgrimage to the famous religious shrine of Santiago de Compostela. He stopped overnight at an inn in the town of Astorga where he got involved in a small drinking party with a frolicsome group of local citizens. At the height of the general merriment, somebody pulled open Benito's knapsack, and out fell a Communion wafer.

Everybody knew what the wafer meant: Benito Garcia was involved in a Jewish Ritual Murder. His companions, smelling a foul crime, seized him and carried him off to Pedro de Villada, the bishop's vicar in Astorga and thus the highest Church official in town. The vicar wasted no time; ignoring Benito's frightened protestations of innocence, he had him given two hundred lashes. When this didn't produce a confession, the vicar resorted to sterner measures. Benito was submitted to the rack, and when that failed to elicit his cooperation, the water torture was applied. But Benito was obstinate and hardened of heart—for he clearly was not innocent—and it took five days more of continuous torture to persuade him to own up to his crime. His resistance finally crumbled and he confessed that he and a group of accomplices—

THE RITUAL MURDER OF LA GUARDIA

both Conversos and Jews—had taken part in a diabolical plot involving a consecrated wafer and the heart of a Christian boy, the object being to concoct a Jewish magic potion that would kill all Christians and enable the Jews to inherit the earth.

The vicar Pedro de Villada sent a report of his findings to Torquemada. There can be no doubt that the latter saw immediately the tremendous possibilities this case offered for achieving his heart's desire—the expulsion of all Jews from Spain. Under any other circumstances the trial would have been conducted by the tribunal at Toledo, which had jurisdiction over the region of La Guardia, where the alleged crime took place. Instead, Torquemada had the case transferred to Segovia, and announced that he intended to look into it personally, through his own representatives especially chosen to investigate the whole affair. And who were these special proxies? In addition to the two regular Inquisitors at Segovia, Torquemada appointed a third, in the person of his Dominican friend and colleague, friar Fernando de Santo Domingo. A member of Torquemada's monastery at Segovia, it was friar Fernando who had dedicated to the Inquisitor General the *Censure and Confutation of the Talmud*, that exercise in Jew-detecting which was so useful for effective prosecution of Conversos. To assist him in his task, friar Fernando called upon the two authors of the *Censure and Confutation*—the physician Antonio de Avila, and friar Alonso Enriquez, also an inmate of the cloister at Segovia. The task of these three experts in Judaism, working by appointment of Torquemada himself, was to examine into all the exciting possibilities presented in the confession of Benito Garcia at Astorga.

By the first of July, 1490, in addition to Benito Garcia, seven "accomplices" whom he had named in his confession had been rounded up on Torquemada's order and jailed at Segovia. Five of them, like Benito, were Conversos from La Guardia, and two were Jews from towns nearby. Almost immediately after their arrival in Segovia, one of the Jewish prisoners—Juce Franco—became so ill that it seemed virtually certain he would die at any moment.

This was a piece of good fortune that could come only from Heaven, and Torquemada's trinity of Jewish experts sought to exploit their opportunity.

Antonio de Avila, in his capacity as physician, descended to the cell of Juce Franco to tend to his needs and also to see if he could pick up any incriminating tidbits for the prosecution. Apparently convinced that death was near, Franco begged Avila to send him a rabbi so that, as he put it, he could "say the things Jews say when they are about to die." As soon as he heard this piece of news, Inquisitor Santo Domingo sent for his Dominican colleague, the former Jew now turned Jew-hunter, friar Alonso Enriquez. The latter donned the garb of a rabbi and, identifying himself to Juce Franco as "rabbi Abraham," he prepared to take the prisoner's deathbed confession, urging the absolute necessity of a complete unburdening of the conscience before God. But all he could get from Juce Franco was the statement that Franco was in jail on a Jewish Ritual Murder charge, which was hardly news. So a week later "rabbi Abraham" tried again, but by this time Juce Franco had become both healthier and suspicious, and refused to tell him anything.

When this pious deception failed of its purpose, Torquemada decided that justice could better be served by transferring the case to the new Dominican monastery he was building at Avila, where he could preside over it in person. Although there was no formal tribunal of the Inquisition at Avila, Torquemada had thoughtfully equipped his new monastery with all the necessary machinery, including an audience chamber, dungeons (which latter, his friends always tell us, were more "light and airy" than the usual dungeon), and a well stocked torture chamber. But a call from the Catholic Kings to join them at the royal court forced Torquemada once again to deny himself the pleasures of personal participation in this case. During his absence, he would make sure that the matter was in good hands. In August, 1490, he appointed three "Inquisitors of Avila," with headquarters in his monastery, and instructed them to leave no heretic unscathed in getting to the bottom of the whole Jewish abomination of La Guardia. The three "Inquisitors of Avila" were a perfect choice for anyone whose sense of scruples readily disintegrates in his enthusiasm for results. One of them was Juan Lopez de Cigales, plucked from the Inquisition tribunal at Valencia, where he had contributed to the mechanics of Jew-detecting the previously discussed *Declaration of the Ceremonies of the Judaic Rites*. The other two Inquisitors were also old friends: Doctor Pedro de Villada, bishop's vicar at Astorga, whose relentless interrogation of Benito Garcia had uncovered the whole diabolical conspiracy, and friar Fernando de Santo Domingo, director of the investigations at Segovia.

The conduct of the trials at Avila is a tribute to that human madness which refuses to let uneasy facts, or the absence of evidence, or patent contradictions, deter the Righteous from the path of Truth. The question was not whether a Ritual Murder had been committed, nor even whether the prisoners on hand were the ones who had committed it. Juce Franco, who was apparently looked upon as the ringleader, insisted that the accusations against him were "the greatest falsehoods in the world." But as time dragged on and the airy solitude of the dungeon was relieved only by repeated questionings under torture, more and more admissions were gradually extracted from the prisoners. Probably the biggest break in the case came in July of 1491 when, after a year and a half of intense effort, the labors of the Inquisitors were rewarded by a confession from Juce Franco. About three years before, he said, he and his fellow prisoners had taken a Christian boy to a cave near La Guardia. There they had crucified him in a cruel mockery of the Passion of Christ, ripping his heart out of his body and draining off his blood. Some time later they reassembled at the scene of the crime. The heart was produced, along with a consecrated wafer. One of the other Jews took these properties to a corner of the cave where he performed certain magic ceremonies which, he assured the others, would protect them from the Inquisition, for any Inquisitor who laid hands on them would turn into a raving maniac before a year was out.

Further prompting during the next few months brought more grisly details. However, there were two sticky problems to be cleared up before the case could be made airtight. First, the identity of the boy martyr had to be established, and a corpus delecti produced. Second, the testimonies of the prisoners conflicted in many details, and needed to be harmonized.

Identifying the boy martyr turned out to be an exercise in frustration. No reports of missing children had been made in La Guardia; no frantic mother had appeared to bewail the loss of a son. Even the prisoners didn't seem to know who their victim was. One of them did finally come up with a name, and identified the missing martyr as the son of one Alonso Martin of the village of Quintanar. Inquiries at Quintanar turned up several Alonso Martins—the name was as common as John Smith is here—but none of them had missed any sons. Another prisoner was persuaded to confess that he had buried the remains. So he was convoyed to the scene at La Guardia to point out the grave. Unfortunately, no body was found, although the officials who inspected the alleged grave reported that it looked as though somebody had dug a hole there. As for the boy's heart, the bulk of the testimony had it that Benito Garcia had been carrying it around in his knapsack, along with the wafer which had started all the trouble. But the heart had not been in the fatal knapsack, and no trace of it could be found anywhere. No heart, no corpse: the Inquisitors would simply have to settle for the wafer.

The efforts of the Inquisitors to reconcile the conflicting testimonies of their prisoners turned into a comedy of errors. In September (1491), all the prisoners were again tortured and asked some leading questions, but their stories still did not harmonize. So on November 2, they were tortured again and asked another series of leading questions, this time prepared carefully in advance. Even then, no agreement could be obtained on the date—or even on the year—when the Ritual Murder was supposed to have taken place. There were even discrepancies on the number of hearts that had been passed around. (Somebody obviously was confessing too hard.) Nor could Torquemada's experts get any kind of a straight story about how the victim was obtained, nor from where, nor just who had obtained him.

The Inquisitors finally gave up the task as hopeless. The inconsistencies of testimony and the disappearance of both heart and cadaver only convinced them that they were dealing with congenital liars as well as Satan's helpers. At a spectacular Auto de Fe on November 16, 1491, the two Jewish prisoners were torn with hot pincers and then burned to death. The corpses of three other Jews who had also been implicated were dug up and burned, together with their effigies. The Conversos, including Benito Garcia, professed repentance for their crime, begging to be taken back into the True Faith. They were therefore mercifully strangled before their bodies were consigned to the flames.

With the execution of his murderers, the boy-saint of La Guardia became a national monument. In his home town, the house of Juce Franco was torn down to make way for the "Church of the Sainted Innocent," appropriately built on the very spot where the plot was hatched. The crucifixion cave and a goodly part of the adjoining real estate became hallowed ground, where miracles were wrought in stunning profusion. The cave itself was refurbished and transformed into a great church, while just outside a monastery was built for the Trinitarian fathers, and three chapels were constructed nearby. A literary tradition quickly sprang up too, and the boy-saint soon became a staple fare in Golden Age drama as well as in numerous piously aggressive narratives down into the present century. According to these accounts, the martyr's name was Christopher. He was stolen by Jews from his blind mother. They built a great big heavy Cross and made him pack it all around the mountain at La Guardia, flogging him either 5,500 or 6,200 times while he did so. Then they dragged him into the cave and crucified him in an elaborate ceremony, one Jew acting out the role of Pontius Pilate, another playing Judas, others standing in for Annas, Caiaphas, Herod, and the whole infernal assembly compromised in the death of

Christ. At the very instant Christopher expired on the Cross, the whole earth trembled, the sun shuddered in its heavenly path, and the martyr's blind old mother miraculously recovered her sight. On the Third Day, his body, with heart restored, ascended into Heaven to join the blessed company of angels, which explains how the heart wriggled out of the knapsack and the body forsook the grave. The single terrestrial exhibit, on which the whole La Guardia case had been so doggedly constructed, was the wafer found in Benito Garcia's knapsack. This was put in a silver casket in Torquemada's monastery church at Avila. Here it performed many miracles, the most notable of which occurred some thirty years after the trial; for several years all of Spain was ravaged by the plague, excepting only Avila, which remained healthy through the intervention of its wafer.

For his part, Torquemada was more concerned with immediate consequences than with the edification of future generations. If Ferdinand and Isabella were hesitating over expelling the Jews from Spain, the discovery of this latest Jewish plot would surely resolve all doubts. The Auto de Fe of November, 1491, exploited the affair to its fullest, emphasizing not only all the gruesome details of the Murder but the Jewish menace to Christians intended by it. The sentence against the Jew Juce Franco, read aloud to the great crowd at the Auto de Fe, identifies him as a seducer of Christians to the Law of Moses in language that clearly foreshadows the Edict of Expulsion four months later:

> *It has been clearly proven* (the condemnation reads) *that the Jew Juce Franco did seduce some Christians to the rites and ceremonies of the Law of Moses by teaching them Jewish prayers, praying in Hebrew to the Creator to whom he commended them, and telling them that the Law of Moses was the true law, whereas the Law of Christ was false.*
>
> *He also taught them the times of the Jewish Passover and other Fasts, and explained to them why the Jews did not eat certain meats. He further did communicate to and participate with these same*

Christians in other mysteries of his Jewish law, serving them Jewish foods and wine, eating and drinking with them the better to confirm them in the Law of Moses.

When the Inquisitors got to Juce Franco's part in the Ritual Murder, they did not disappoint the morbid tastes of the spectators at the Auto de Fe.

This Juce Franco personally took part, together with other Jews and with Christians, in the crucifixion—at night and in a secret cave—of an innocent Christian boy. They stretched out his arms and legs on two boards arranged in the form of a Cross. Then they flogged him, spat on him, beat him, tore out the pieces of his flesh and put a crown of thorns on his head.

This Juce Franco, with his own hands seized the bleeding boy by the arm, cut open his side with a knife and took out his heart. Then he beat him and tore his flesh in memory and vituperation of the Sacred Passion of Jesus Christ our Redeemer, uttering curses and insults on the Person of Christ as though He were actually on the Cross. And while they were flogging the said youth, they said to him: "This traitor and deceiver, when he preached, spoke lies against the Law of God and the Law of Moses. Now you will pay for the things you said and did in that ancient time. You thought you would abase us and exalt yourself, for which you shall suffer even more evil than this. You thought you would destroy us, but we will destroy you. Crucify him, crucify him—this dog, this swindler, this deceiver and bewitcher! He called himself King of the Jews. But he was a mere man, like any other, a bastard born in adultery, the son of a corrupt and adulterous woman. He tried to destroy the Jews and their Law, but it is he who will be destroyed by us, for coming to turn the Jews into Christians with his deceptions and witchcraft."

These words and vituperations (the Inquisition sentence goes on) *this Franco and the other Jews first taught to these Christians, who then imitated these Jews in the same manner, repeating the same vituperations and others of the same kind.*

And after the child had been tortured and crucified by this Juce Franco and the others, they killed him, took him down from the Cross, and took him away and secretly buried him that same night where no one could find him. Some days later this Jew, Juce Franco, and all his other accomplices in this crime, met together secretly in the same cave, where they performed certain conjuring and experiments in witchcraft with the heart of the dead boy and a consecrated Communion wafer. They performed these conjurings with the perverted and diabolical intention of making the Inquisitors against heretical depravity together with all other Christians go mad and die of madness, and of subverting, and destroying and killing the Holy Faith of Jesus Christ our Redeemer, exalting the Law of Moses and making the Jews lords over all.

We may be sure that Ferdinand and Isabella were treated to a lengthy account of this case. It also is clear, from their own observations in the Edict of Expulsion, that Torquemada impressed on them the determination of the Jews to persist in their efforts to seduce Christians to Judaism. As long as they were permitted to remain, the danger of infection would never be eliminated, no matter how harsh the measures employed against them.

The reluctance of the Crown to take such drastic action was finally overcome. In January, 1492, Spanish armies completed the conquest (and purification) of the realm by capturing the city of Granada, last stronghold of the Moorish power which had flooded into the Peninsula over seven centuries before. It was appropriate, therefore, that the ancient palace of the Infidel—the Alhambra in Granada—should provide the setting where the fate of Spain's Jews was irrevocably sealed, and the lifelong dream of Thomas de Torquemada now came true.[1]

---

[1] No doubt the Jews did all they could to dissuade the Crown from expelling them. Certainly the royal financial adviser Don Abraham Seneor must have exerted his considerable influence to protect his co-religionists from the threatened disaster. There is a legend, often repeated as fact by historians of this period, that the Jews tried to buy off the Crown with a bribe of thirty thousand pieces of

THE RITUAL MURDER OF LA GUARDIA   127

On March 31, 1492, Ferdinand and Isabella announced to the world that there were some "bad Christians" in Spain who were rejecting the True Faith to return to Judaism. The Jews themselves were responsible for this, for they simply would not give up their efforts to subvert the Faith. The royal patience had for years limited itself to preventive measures: Jews had been expelled from a few cities; in others they had been required to live in ghettos, where they could not contaminate their Christian neighbors. Finally, only twelve years before, the Crown had established the Holy Office of the Inquisition to root out such heresies all over Spain. And, "as is well known, through its efforts many guilty persons have been found out."

But just recently, their Highnesses observed, they had been informed by the Inquisitors that the Jews were still continuing their evil ways,

> *seducing faithful Christians to their own damnable beliefs and opinions, instructing them in the ceremonies and observances of the Jewish law, holding meetings where they read to them and teach them what to believe, advising them of the Jewish Fast days to observe, teaching them the histories of their law, instructing them about the Passover and other Jewish ceremonies, supplying them with unleavened bread and ceremonially prepared meats and persuading them to observe the Law of Moses, giving them to understand that there is no true law except the Law of Moses.*

It had become clear, therefore, that nothing would dissuade the Jews from their war against the True Faith except their removal, root and branch, from the realm of the Faithful. And so their

---

gold, and that Ferdinand and Isabella were seriously considering the offer. At this critical juncture, Torquemada is said to have thrust his way into the royal chamber and shamed his hesitant employers with an embarrassing reference to Judas and his thirty pieces of silver. Although the story has no basis in fact it serves to illustrate that Torquemada was the kind of man about whom legends would inevitably be concocted. History and legend are not necessarily antagonistic. The latter often provides us with an insight into the attitudes of contemporaries toward a man or an event.

Highnesses were forced, by the actions of the Jews themselves, to adopt the most drastic measures for the safety of Christendom.

> *To this end we hereby issue this our Edict, by virtue of which we command all Jews, of both sexes and all ages, who live, dwell, and are in any way present in our kingdoms and lands, both natives and foreigners who in whatever manner or for whatever reason have come or are now here, that by the end of July of this present year of 1492, they be gone from all our kingdoms and lands, together with their sons, daughters, Jewish servants and familiars, without regard to rank or station, and of whatever age they may be, and that they not presume to return or even to pass through these realms nor any part of them under pain of death and confiscation of all their property.*

The destiny of a whole race was thus turned into an odyssey of horror by a few strokes of the royal pen. Behind it lay the accumulated hatred of generations of purifiers speaking in the voice of Torquemada.

CHAPTER 12

The Wandering Jew

I begged and pleaded until my throat was hoarse. I implored the king: "PLEASE," *I begged him,* "do not force such a terrible act on your subjects. Impose hardships on us: gifts of gold and silver and all they possess will the Israelites gladly give you if only you will allow them to remain in their native land."

I implored my friends who enjoyed the royal favor to intercede for my people. They held a council and agreed to speak to the king to persuade him to withdraw his savage order and abandon his project to exterminate the Jews. But like a deaf viper he stopped up his ears and would not change his mind. Also, the queen remained at his side to see that he did not change his mind, and she used the most powerful persuasions to make him carry the task to its conclusion. We worked with frenzy, but without success. I had no peace or rest. The disaster fell upon us.

So wrote Isaac Abravanel, colleague of Abraham Seneor and like him, a favored adviser of the Catholic Kings.

The Jews had four months to leave Spain. The original deadline of July 31 was moved forward to August 2, a grim coincidence for the Israelites. August 2, 1492, fell on the ninth day of the Jewish month of Ab. According to Jewish tradition, this day was a double anniversary of the destruction of the first Temple of Jerusalem by the Babylonians in 586 B.C. and of the second Temple by the Romans in 70 A.D. It was, and still is today, a day of mourning for orthodox Jews all over the world.

While the dazed Jews began preparing for their exit, Christian missionaries descended on the ghettos, preaching salvation from disaster through union with the Redeemer. The Jews were required by law to attend their exhortations. They listened, but they did not hear. The People's historian Andres Bernaldez, who will be at our elbow (as he was at the Jews') during the first stages of the new diaspora, was indignant at this stiff-necked attitude.

Before their very eyes (he writes) *they could see their own ruin and exile. And even though they were urged and admonished by preachings and exhortations, they persisted in their pertinacity and unbelief and refused to accept the opportunity held out to them. Instead, when the preaching of the Evangel concluded, their rabbis preached the opposite, filling them with vain hopes. They told them that their exile was an act of God, who had decided to free them from captivity and take them to the Promised Land and that God would perform many miracles for them and guide them across the sea as He had done with their ancestors in Egypt. Under no circumstances were the Jews willing to convert, except for a very few of the most hard-pressed.*

The most hard-pressed Jew of all was Don Abraham Seneor. Most of us, fortunately, can coast through life without having to face up to the horrors of self-revelation. But History played a cruel trick on the royal Jew. Ferdinand and Isabella alternately pleaded and threatened. The Jewish community was silent, waiting and watching. Don Abraham had to decide between hard principle and damnable expediency. He waited to the end, hoping in vain for a way out. Finally, he resigned himself, with death in his soul, to baptism and Christian brotherhood with Torquemada, scourge of his own people.

In Segovia the Jewish community succumbed to a collective

compulsion. They literally went underground, carving out large caverns among the tombs of their fathers in the local cemetery, hoping to hide out there and somehow avoid expulsion. They were soon discovered and rooted out of their caves. A few accepted baptism; the others joined the weary march of their comrades, preferring exile to the conversion which brought Torquemada's Inquisition in its baggage train.

Ye cannot serve God and mammon, says the Gospel. But a man could hardly be expected to turn his back when mammon was standing at the right hand of the Lord. The Jews were allowed to take with them only what they could carry, except for gold and silver, the most important equipment for survival in strange lands. Their Christian debtors, of course, wrote off all their obligations. The clergy made preparations to transform the synagogues into churches. Some municipal governments agreed to accept deeds to Jewish cemeteries for use as pasturage, and promised to leave the dead undisturbed. Others simply waited until the Jews were gone and then confiscated their burial grounds for local real estate needs. Wonderful bargains were to be had in Jewish houses and land, and Bernaldez tells us that the market price for a house was a mule, while a whole vineyard could be bought for a piece of cloth or linen. In many instances it was impossible even to get that kind of price and some Jews burned their houses down to the ground rather than let them fall into waiting Christian hands. This was only a petulant minority, however, and as soon as the Jews left, their Christian neighbors took over their houses and lands. The Catholic Kings were sorely vexed over this, because abandoned property rightfully belonged to the Crown, and private expropriation amounted to illegal theft. After the Jews had gone, King Ferdinand began a thorough investigation to determine what Jewish property had been usurped from the Crown. He even addressed lengthy inquiries to the authorities in the many places where the exiles had settled, asking them to solicit the cooperation of the Jews in the interests of justice.

By July the roads of Spain were choked with Jewish columns reliving the memories of Egypt.[1] Some slipped across the northern border into the small (and unfriendly) kingdom of Navarre, only to be expelled from there six years later. Others bought the uncertain sufferance of the king of Portugal but ultimately were massacred and driven from that country too. The main army headed for the seaports of the east and south. They staggered along, says Bernaldez, "big and small, old and young, on foot, on horseback, mounted on asses, riding in carts, stumbling and falling and getting up again, some sick, others dying, and new ones being born." Through town and country, Christians came to watch, calling on them to save themselves now and forever in the forgiving arms of the Redeemer. But the rabbis moved among them urging them to hold fast, lacing their exhortations with allusions to Egypt and the Red Sea and the Promised Land of milk and honey. And the women and children sang and beat their tambourines to keep up their courage.

When they saw the sea at Cadiz, says Bernaldez, the Jews "gave a great shout, crying out to God for mercy." For hours they stared at the waters, waiting for the Lord to part the Mediterranean. But Jehovah stayed His hand, and they embarked on a flotilla of vessels waiting to carry them to North Africa.[2]

The blue Mediterranean became a death trap for many. Sea rovers attacked their ships, plundered them and threw their victims

---

[1] Estimates of the number of exiles begin at 100,000 and stop at 800,000. The mean is around 400,000.

[2] The morning after the last Jews departed, the three caravels of Christopher Columbus sailed out of the Gulf of Cadiz on their way to the New World. On board was a ship's physician named Maestro Bernal. A Converso, Bernal had been penanced as a secret Judaizer in an Auto de Fe at Valencia in 1490. Also with Columbus was Luis de Torres, a recently baptized Jew who apparently chose the perils of the unknown as his way of escape. Torres was a man of much linguistic talent, and is said to have been an expert in Eastern languages. Columbus hired him to serve as his interpreter between the Spaniards and the exotic aborigines they might encounter. Torres never returned to Spain; instead, he settled down for the rest of his life among the natives of Cuba, who cared little about his religious idiosyncrasies.

into the sea. Storms scattered their fleets, and their ship captains dumped them on the beaches of North Africa, where roving Berber tribesmen swopped down on them, killing the men and carrying off the women. At the African ports of Oran and Algiers the inhabitants, who objected to the threatened overcrowding of their cities, attacked the fugitives, wounding and killing many of them as they disembarked.

A large body of exiles struck inland for the Moroccan capital at Fez, eighty-five miles to the south. After a harrowing march through a hostile land, abused by the elements and freebooting Berbers, they climbed up the rolling hills about Fez, where the olive gardens and orange groves of the city stretched out before them. But the city gates were closed against them, for the same "practical" reasons that impel modern nations to protect their economic integrity against the influx of the earth's disinherited. So the Jews camped in the fields, feeding on grass and roots like cattle. The modern Jewish historian Heinrich Graetz tells us that on the Sabbath they stripped the plants with their teeth, so as not to violate the holy day by gathering them. Fathers sold their children as slaves for a loaf of bread, and mothers killed their infants rather than see them die of hunger.

It was more than the Jews could bear. They would return to the land of their birth rather than die like starving animals far from home. Somehow they did get back, and our priestly historian, Andres Bernaldez, was on hand to baptize the repentant prodigals and record the miracle of their return:

They came back barefooted and naked and crawling with lice. Along the way they were plundered by the Moors, who stripped them to the skin, raping the women and killing the men. They ran their fingers inside their mouths and in the women's lower regions and cut open their victims' bellies looking for the gold the Jews were known to have hidden on their persons. And the women told of other ugly things which those brute animals had done to them— things it were better not to describe here. Finding themselves once again free in the land of civilized people, they gave thanks to God for having led them out of their sufferings among such beasts. Behold the dishonor, the calamities and the grievous punishments He has visited upon this generation of Moses for their wicked unbelief and the obstinate pride with which they deny the Savior and true Messiah, our Lord and Redeemer Jesus Christ, whose arms are always open to receive them. But never before, until now, when compelled to do so by disaster, have they been willing to accept Him. But now we are witness to the fulfilling of the prophecy of King David when he said of wicked transgressors: "They return at evening; they make a noise like a dog and go round about the city."

With the words of King David and Father Bernaldez still ringing in our ears, we leave our priestly guide at this point to pick up with a young Jewish boy whose history is preserved for us in the records of the Inquisition at Valencia. Luis de la Isla was eight years old when he took up the tambourine on the long road to Cadiz. Somewhere in the horrors of North Africa he apparently became separated from his parents and began a lifetime of wandering in search of them. For two months he tramped the Barbary Coast without success, and finally slipped aboard a ship bound with a load of refugees for Italy. Italian sea captains had already acquired a reputation for brutality toward Jewish exiles, robbing them and flinging them into the sea for the sheer sport of murdering the helpless and downtrodden.

The Italian cities swarmed with Jewish refugees. Pope Alexander VI, whose scandalous life even today chills the hearts of the Faithful, set a tolerant example by allowing the Jews freely to enter Rome. Other cities either followed or ignored the papal precedent according to local sentiments too complex for the human mind to unravel. For four years young Luis wandered through Italy. We catch brief glimpses of him in Venice and finally in Genoa where, by his own account, he became a convert to Christianity. It is only from other sources that we learn something of these strange circumstances: the republic of Genoa forbade Jews to remain within its boundaries for more than three days. Baptism nullified the ban, of course, and the starving Jewish children who haunted the streets were rewarded with a loaf of bread for opening their hearts to the Savior.

Perhaps his parents had returned to Spain with the naked remnant from Fez. Luis de la Isla, now twelve years old and a nominal Christian, went back to his homeland. For ten years he moved from city to city, working at irregular intervals as a weaver of textiles. Four times he returned to Toledo, near to his boyhood home at Illescas. In 1506, now twenty-two, he returned to Italy and visited Rome, Bologna and Ferrara, where the narrative of his odyssey begins to fill out. He applied for work at the shop of a Spanish Jewish exile who now ran a prosperous millinery in Ferrara:

> *He asked me about my previous experience in this kind of work. He also asked me where I came from. I told him I was a Castilian, a native of Illescas, that I had formerly been a Jew and was now a Christian.*

The Jew courted Luis for two weeks, trying to woo him back to the synagogue. Nothing came of it except that Luis declined to return to Judaism and his new friend decided he already had all the help he needed at the shop. Luis set out for Venice to try his luck in the lands of the Grand Turk.

In those days the domain of the Sultan spread from the Balkan States on the Adriatic eastward through Turkey and Asia Minor, and south into the ancient kingdom of Egypt. The Sultan welcomed Spain's Jews, and vast numbers of them found happy refuge in the great cities of the East. Under Turkish law they were protected against the many oppressions which had made their lives miserable in Spain. The Sultan not only invited the Jews to settle on his lands, but he further insulted Spanish honor by publicly doubting the legendary wisdom of the Catholic Kings who drove such an industrious people from Spain. The royal tutor, Peter Martyr, was so stung by this slur on the reputations of

Ferdinand and Isabella that he hastened to inform the world that the Sultan was a blind fool just asking for trouble:

> *If the Sultan knew how diseased these Jews are, how pestiferous and contagious, he would drive them from Egypt a second time as happened in the days of Pharaoh. By their touch alone they spread dirt. They corrupt everything they look upon. Their words destroy everyone. They upset everything human and divine. If the Sultan lives long enough he will come to realize what kind of people he has mixed with his own, and how filthy and cursed and vile and abominable they are, worthy only of being removed from all contact with humanity. Then he would have to admit the wisdom of the Catholic Kings in driving out such cattle.*

In Venice, the abominable Luis hired himself out as a servant to a pair of abominable Portuguese merchants and they sailed together across the Adriatic to the port of Aulona in Turkish Albania. The three confessed their Jewish origins to one another and cemented their bond by spending the Lenten season at Aulona eating meat and unleavened bread in celebration of the Passover.

A band of Jewish exiles passing through Aulona on their way to new homes in the East, brought tales of friends and kinsmen from Spain who had found a new life in the cities of Greece and Asia Minor. Luis declared himself to be a Jew, took the name of Abraham, and joined them in a caravan of Jews, Greeks and Turks headed for Constantinople. In Salonika, Adrianople, and other cities on the way, he found old acquaintances from Spain who told him about others of his countrymen in places still farther on. From Constantinople, against the advice of the Jews there, he struck out alone. Southward he wandered around the western crescent of the Sea of Marmora and across the cruel sands of "Old Turkey" to lonely desert towns with strange names. At Kutayah a Spanish Jew from Castile spoke of others who had passed that way for the southern coast and beyond, to Cyprus and Egypt. From Antalya he crossed the Eastern Mediterranean and landed in Alexandria. Soon after his arrival there, he fell ill. When he recovered, he was blind.

Luis da la Isla decided to go home. In 1512 he was back in Toledo at the scenes of his childhood. He was a sick, blind old man. He was twenty-eight. Soon after, he was seized by the Inquisition. The records of his trial break off at the year 1514, at which time he was languishing in a dungeon at Toledo. We never hear of him again.

CHAPTER 13

The Messiah Cometh

ON MARCH 23, 1494, Ferdinand and Isabella transferred the royal title to the Jewish cemetery at Avila to the Dominican fathers, and authorized them to use the tombstones for construction work. On the year of his ascension as General of the Holy Office, Torquemada had begun the building of the monastery of Saint Thomas in Avila. Under his personal supervision it had grown into an imposing compound of buildings designed for pious mediations and Inquisitorial purification. A tribunal of the Holy Office was established at the new monastery in 1490 to avenge the Ritual Murder of the boy saint of La Guardia. Torquemada came to cherish his Avila monastery at home, and he took a special interest in the operations of its small but thorough Inquisition. He dominated it completely until his death in 1498, and a few simple statistics tell of the spirit he breathed into it.

Everybody has a suggestion but nobody really knows the number of victims purged by the Inquisition in the time of Torquemada. Thousands, tens of thousands, and perhaps more, were given punishments ranging from small fines to life imprisonment. Early in the nineteenth century, the secretary of the Spanish Inquisition, Juan Antonio Llorente, defected to France with a cartload of documents. Soon after, he published at Paris an unsympathetic history of that organization, which the Faithful still denounce today as a pack of lies. Among other unkind cuts was the author's announcement that Torquemada and his men had burned upwards of nine thousand persons at the stake in eight years. The "spiteful exaggerations" of Llorente have been revised downward and some of Torquemada's modern friends assure us that (a) he really burned only two thousand human beings, and (b) the actual execution of the death sentence was performed by the secular arm of the government, for "the Church does not shed blood." Without venturing further into this swamp of statistics and dialectics, we may reasonably guess that (a) burning accounted for some five percent of the total, and (b) that Torquemada took a lively interest in the proceedings.

At Avila, however, the quality of mercy was carefully strained. Three centuries after Torquemada's passing, the penitential garments of Avila's heretics were still hanging in the monastery for future sinners to contemplate. These garments were worn at the Auto de Fe, and bore elaborate designs indicating the nature of the sinner's impending punishment. After the Auto they were placed in a local trophy room, with the names of their wearers inscribed on them to preserve their infamy for Posterity. A count taken in the nineteenth century showed that of 158 persons who appeared before the Avila tribunal under Torquemada, eighty-nine were burned at the stake, slightly over fifty-six percent of the total. Also, for the century after Torquemada's death, burnings took place once every seven years, compared with once every month in the earlier period.

The Pope, whose orthodoxy is unimpeachable, had firm doubts about Torquemada's wisdom as an administrator. In 1494, citing numerous complaints about the latter's zealous irregularities, he tried to clip the Inquisitor General's wings by packing the Holy Office with four additional appointees of equal rank. But Torquemada's reputation, and the Crown's support, guaranteed him first place among his new peers, and his authority remained undiminished to the end.

Torquemada died in the odor of sanctity September 16, 1498, in the monastery of Saint Thomas at Avila. The lamentations of the Faithful mingled with the excited hosannas of the Conversos who saw the hand of Jehovah reaching into Avila to slay the Great Leviathan and lead the children of Israel into the Promised Land. It was foretold in the writings of the rabbis that the Righteous would feed on the flesh of the Monster on the eve of the coming of the True Messiah. The signs were there for all to see: the Great Leviathan was dead; the century of wrath was spinning out its destiny. The Messiah would come in 1500.

Latter-day prophets suddenly appeared from the northern frontier to Cordova in the south and Valencia in the east. The small village of Herrera near the French border became a Mecca for Conversos as far away as Madrid and Toledo. A shoemaker's daughter named Inez was making weekly ascensions into Heaven and returning with olive branches, carnations, letters from Yahweh, and advance reports on the coming of the Messiah. There she saw the souls of all those who had been burned at the stake by Torquemada. They were now living in abundance and glory, sitting in golden chairs and eating from golden plates. Meanwhile, God was building a wonderful city where all the Conversos would live forever in the land of milk and honey. On the appointed day the sky would turn copper, the prophet Elijah would descend on a cloud to preach of redemption, with the Messiah right behind him to lead the way into the Promised Land. For the next seven years no rain would fall on the earth below. Those who wished to make the trip must return immediately to the Law of Moses. They need no longer fear the Inquisition, for they would soon be beyond its reach.

The revelations of Inez were quickly confirmed by some of her disciples. A butcher reported a conversation with his dead father-in-law who stepped from the beyond to tell of the discomforts he was suffering for having neglected the Mosaic Law. A neighbor lady spoke with her dead father who also urged the future merits of Mosaic custom. A young girl stumbled on Abraham and Moses in the family parlor and they corroborated the reports about the forthcoming trip to the Promised Land. So the Conversos gave away their worldly goods, scanned the heavens for the promised signs, and began dancing in the streets, singing "Tomorrow we go to the Promised Land." Inez was decked out in jewels and fine clothing in preparation for her marriage with the Prince of Judea who was waiting in Heaven to wed her when she arrived with her friends.

In the village of Chillon a peasant girl named Maria announced that she too had made a recent trip to Heaven where she was informed that all Conversos who observed the Mosaic Law would be carried off to the Promised Land. The citizens there followed the example of their brethren at Herrera by openly returning to Judaism in celebration of the coming salvation. A wool-carder named Gomez began holding seances at the town of Almodovar on Thursday and Sunday evenings. His spirit would travel across country to visit with Inez and Maria, and then up to Heaven to see God, Elijah, and the Messiah. There he learned that one day soon a great thunderclap would split the heavens and Elijah would descend to lead the Conversos into the Promised Land, where seven thousand handsome young men were waiting to marry the earthbound local maidens, and six young virgins were on hand to wed Gomez and his five fellow-prophets, who are otherwise not identified. The sinners marked out for salvation had already been chosen and their names revealed to Gomez who would assign them their lodgings with a wave of his golden wand.

At Valencia, Moses himself was reincarnated in the person of one Miguel Vives, where he was preparing once again to lead the Jews (i.e., Conversos) out of the Spanish Egypt and into the New Canaan. And when the Chosen People were rolled up in the heavenly scroll, the Lord would visit His vengeance upon their persecutors. Spain would be ravaged by famine, war, disease and death. The beasts of the field would roam the streets of her deserted cities. And the dogs would eat of their flesh and lick the blood of their bones.

The Messiah never came, but the familiars of the Inquisition did. While the prophets and their followers perished in the flames, the Great Leviathan slumbered on in a crypt in the chapel of Saint Thomas at Avila. His bones were removed to a more elaborate tomb in 1579 amidst hushed talk about their delicately sweet odor of apparent supernatural origin. In the nineteenth century, during one of those rare spasms of Liberal Reform which momentarily upset the medieval pattern of Spanish life, the Inquisition was finally abolished. Two years later (1836), Liberal grave-robbers with an ironic sense of history broke open Torquemada's tomb at Avila. They took out his bones, burned them on the spot where his victims had perished before him, and cast his ashes to the winds.

Index

Abenbilla, Mayr . . . 96
Abolafia, Samuel . . . 114
Abraham the Jew . . . 16
Abravanel, Isaac . . . 129
Adamuz . . . 65
Adrianople . . . 136
Aguilar, Alonso de . . . 65
Albania . . . 136
Alexander VI . . . 134
Alexandria . . . 137
Alfonso, Fernando . . . 111
Alfonso III (Spain) . . . 24
Alfonso X (Spain) . . . 24, 25–7
Algiers . . . 133
Alhambra, the . . . 126
Almodovar del Campo . . . 65, 141
Altas, Ribas . . . 113
Alva, duke of . . . 113
Alvarez, Juan . . . 96–7
American Jewish Yearbook . . . 12n
Andalusia . . . 65, 113
Annas . . . 123
Antequera, Ferdinand of . . . 42
Antichrist . . . 53, 54, 56–8, 113
Aquitania . . . 5
Aragon . . . 23, 24, 46, 50, 51, 61, 64, 80–1
Aranda, Pedro de . . . 77–8
Arbues, Pedro . . . 81
Arevalo, Nuño de . . . 106–9
Asia Minor . . . 19, 135, 136
Astorga . . . 118, 119, 121
Aulona . . . 136
Austria (persecution of Jews) . . . 7, 8
Avignon . . . 51n
Avila . . . 39, 73, 75, 113, 120ff., 138, 139, 140, 142
Avila, Antonio de . . . 85, 119, 120
Aztecs . . . 11

Barbary Coast . . . 39
Barcelona . . . 38–9, 48, 81, 112
Bardaxi, Brianda de . . . 99–102
Basle . . . 9
Bavaria . . . 8
beata de Piedrahita (see Santo Domingo, Maria de)
Belgium (persecution of Jews) . . . 17
Benedict XIII . . . 51
Berbers . . . 133
Bernal, Maestro . . . 132n
Bernaldez, Andres . . . 60–1, 72, 130ff.
Bilbao . . . 114
Black Death . . . 8–9, 30, 56

Blois . . . 13–14
Bologna . . . 135
Book of the Cabala . . . 16
book-burning . . . 78–9
Boppard . . . 15
Bordeaux . . . 7
Boston (Mass.) . . . 12
Bray . . . 6
Bristol . . . 13
Brussels . . . 17
Burgos . . . 47, 72, 77, 114
Burgos, Abner of (see Valladolid, Alfonso de)
Burgundy, duke of . . . 57
Bury St. Edmunds . . . 13

Caballeria, Pedro de la . . . 52
Cadiz . . . 132
Cadiz, marquis of . . . 68–70
Caiaphas . . . 123
Calahorra . . . 77
Calatrava, order of . . . 47
Calixtus III . . . 40
Calvin, John . . . 76
Canterbury Tales . . . 15, 29n
Cardena . . . 25
Cartagena . . . 47
Caspian Mountains . . . 54
Castile . . . 23, 24, 28–9, 32, 41–2, 46, 61, 62–3, 64, 65, 106, 112, 136
Censure and Confutation of the Talmud . . . 85ff., 119
Chaucer . . . 15, 29n
Chesterton, G. K. . . . 77
Chillon . . . 141
Chronicle of Don Alvaro de Luna . . . 61
Chronicle of the Cid . . . 25
Ciudad Real . . . 39, 102–3, 105, 106, 107, 108
Cluny (monastery) . . . 4
Cologne . . . 5, 15, 17
Columbus, Christopher . . . 47, 132n
Constantine . . . 21, 22, 23, 46
Constantinople . . . 136
Copin . . . 14–15
Cordova . . . 22, 34, 47, 65, 72, 77, 97, 116, 140
Coria . . . 47
Crusades . . . 3–4, 8, 12
Cuba . . . 132n
Cuenca . . . 113
Davila, Juan . . . 80
Der Sturmer . . . 12n

d'Escouchy, Mathieu . . . 56–7

Dominican order . . . 39, 40, 42, 83, 113, 138
Durango . . . 81

Ecija . . . 65
Edward I (England) . . . 6
Egypt . . . 136–7
El Greco . . . 74
England (persecution of Jews) . . . 6, 12, 13
Enriquez, Alonso . . . 85, 119, 120
Enriquez, Juana . . . 47n
Erfurt . . . 7
Espina, Alonso de . . . 52–4, 56, 59, 62, 65, 76, 106, 112

Ferdinand and Isabella . . . 47, 60, 63, 64–5, 66, 67–8, 69, 72, 78, 79, 98, 112, 113–4, 116–7, 120, 124, 126–8, 129, 131, 135–6, 138
Ferrara . . . 135
Fez . . . 133, 135
Flanders . . . 66
Fortress of the Faith . . . 52–4, 55
France (persecution of Jews) . . . 5, 6–7, 13–4, 17, 34, 35
Franciscan order . . . 62
Franco, Juce . . . 119ff.
Franconia . . . 8
Frankfurt . . . 9

Garcia, Benito . . . 118ff.
Gascogne . . . 7
Geneva . . . 8
Genoa . . . 134–5
Germany (persecution of Jews) . . . 4–5, 7–8, 15, 17
Gerona . . . 35
Geronomite order . . . 47, 62, 106, 116
Ghent . . . 57
Gibraltar . . . 66
Gideon . . . 37
Gloucester . . . 13
Gog and Magog . . . 54
Gomez the seer . . . 141
Graetz, Heinrich . . . 133
Granada . . . 22, 34, 47, 69n, 78, 117, 126
Greece . . . 10, 136
Guadalupe . . . 105–6, 107, 108, 116

Haiti . . . 11
Halevi, Solomon (see Santa Maria, Pablo de)
Hamilton, Lady . . . 71
Harold of Gloucester . . . 13

Henry III (England) . . . 14–5
Henry III (Spain) . . . 47
Henry IV (Spain) . . . 47, 62–3, 66, 106, 112
Henry of Trastamara . . . 28–9, 32
Henry the Invalid . . . 42
Herod . . . 123
Herrera . . . 140–1
History of the Catholic Kings . . . 60–1 (see also Bernaldez, Andres)
Hitler, Adolf . . . 47n
Huesca . . . 115–6
Hugh of Lincoln . . . 14–5
Hundred Years War . . . 8, 57n

Ibrahim ibn Ahmed . . . 11
Illescas . . . 135
Incas . . . 11
Inez the seeress . . . 140–1
Isaac . . . 10
Ishmaelites . . . 55
Isla, Luis de la . . . 134–7
Italy . . . 66, 134–5 (anti-Semitism) 26

Jaen . . . 116
Jerez . . . 65, 113
Jerusalem . . . 35, 57, 91, 130
John I (Spain) . . . 32
John II (Spain) . . . 42, 112
Judas . . . 123

Kutayah . . . 136

LaGuardia . . . 118ff., 138
La Rambla . . . 65
La Sisla (monastery) . . . 49–50, 77
Leopard man of the Cameroons . . . 11
Lerida . . . 37
Lilith . . . 11
Llorente, Juan Antonio . . . 138–9
Loire River . . . 13–4
London . . . 6
Lincoln . . . 14–5
Lopez de Cigales, Juan . . . 121ff.
Lorca, Joshua (see Santa Fe, Geronimo de)
Louis VII (France) . . . 4

Maccabees . . . 49
Machiavelli . . . 69n
Madrid . . . 140
Madrid, Juan de . . . 50
Maimonides . . . 34
Mainz . . . 5, 9, 15
Mallorca . . . 50
Maria the seeress . . . 141
Martin, Alonso . . . 122

INDEX

Martin of Aragon . . . 36
Martinez, Ferdinand . . . 31–4, 36, 43, 52, 65, 76, 112
Martyr, Peter . . . 135–6
Massena (New York) . . . 12n
Mather, Cotton . . . 11–2
Medina-Sidonia, duke of . . . 66
Mediterranean Sea . . . 34, 132–3
Mesha, King . . . 10
Mexico . . . 11
Meyer Alguades . . . 42
Midianites . . . 55
Moab . . . 10
Mohammed . . . 22, 91
Montaigne . . . 110
Montoro . . . 65
Moors . . . 22–3, 24, 25, 39, 52, 78, 113, 116, 117, 126, 133
Morillo, Miguel de . . . 68
mystery religions . . . 20

Najara . . . 29
Navarre . . . 29, 132
Nazis . . . 12n
Nebuchadnezzar . . . 18
Nero . . . 20–1
New Mexico . . . 84n
New World . . . 11, 84n, 132n
North Africa . . . 22, 39, 48, 132–4
Northampton . . . 6
Norwich . . . 13
Nuñez, Beatriz . . . 105–9
Nuremberg . . . 8

Odin . . . 10
Ojeda, Alonso de . . . 66–7, 69, 71
Olligoyen, Pedro . . . 29–30
Oran . . . 133
Ordinances of 1412 . . . 43–4, 112
Orthodoxy . . . 77n

Pacheco, Juan . . . 47
Palma . . . 37, 65, 66
Pampano, Juan . . . 103
Pampano, Maria . . . 103–5
Paris . . . 6, 17, 138
Paris, University of . . . 56–7
Peña, Antonio de la . . . 114
Perpignan . . . 35
Persia . . . 22
Peru . . . 11
Peter IV (Spain) . . . 50
Peter the Cruel . . . 28–9, 32
Peter the Venerable . . . 4
Philip Augustus . . . 6
Philo of Byblus . . . 10
Phoenicians . . . 19

Piedrahita . . . 73
Poem of the Cid . . . 24–5
Pontius Pilate . . . 19, 123
Portugal (persecution of Jews) . . . 132
Posen . . . 17–8
Prince Juan . . . 113
Promised Land . . . 72, 132, 140ff.
Pyrenees . . . 30, 34, 35

Queen Catalina . . . 42–3
Quintanar . . . 122

Rasputin . . . 24
Rhine River . . . 7, 9, 15, 17
Richard I (England) . . . 6
Rindfleisch . . . 8
Ritual Murders . . . 6, 9–18, 26, 27, 42, 52, 67, 112, 118–28, 138
Roman Empire . . . 19–21, 22
Roman Inquisition . . . 61
Rome . . . 55, 67, 77, 80, 135
Rottingen . . . 8

Saint Paul . . . 20, 22
Saint Peter . . . 20
Saint Thomas (monastery) . . . 138, 140, 142 (also see Avila)
Saint Vincent Ferrer . . . 40–4, 52, 77
Salonika . . . 136
San Angelo, castle of . . . 78
San Martin, Juan de . . . 68
San Pablo (monastery) . . . 67, 73
Sanchez, Diego . . . 78
Sanchez, Francisco . . . 106–7
Sanchez, Maria . . . 78
Santa Cruz (monastery) . . . 75, 117, 119 (also see Segovia)
Santa Fe, Francisco de . . . 82
Santa Fe, Geronimo de . . . 51–2, 82
Santa Maria, Gonzalo de . . . 77
Santa Maria, Pablo de . . . 52
Santangel, Luis de . . . 47
Santiago, order of . . . 47
Santiago de Compostela . . . 118
Santo Domingo, Fernando de . . . 85, 119ff.
Santo Domingo, Maria de . . . 73n
Saracens . . . 3, 4
Saragossa . . . 81, 84, 99–102, 110, 116
Scrutinium Scripturarum . . . 52
Sea of Marmora . . . 136
Second Coming . . . 86, 116, 138ff.
Segovia . . . 42, 66, 72, 75, 80, 85, 91, 106, 112, 114, 119, 121, 130–1
Seneor, Abraham . . . 64, 112, 114, 117, 126n, 129, 130
Sepulveda . . . 112

Severn River ... 13
Seville ... 22, 31–4, 35, 37, 66, 67, 68, 70–2, 75, 77, 78, 79, 80, 89, 96–7, 112, 116
Sicily ... 11
Siete Partidas ... 25–7
Simon of Trent ... 26
Sinzig ... 7
Sixtus IV ... 67
Solomon Alami ... 43
Speyer ... 5
Strassburg ... 9
Streicher, Julius ... 12n
Sultan of Turkey ... 116, 135–6
Svengali ... 24
Sweden ... 10
Switzerland (persecution of Jews) ... 8, 9
synagogue of Satan ... 52

Tacitus ... 20–1
Talmud ... 52
Teruel ... 40, 81
Tezcatlipoca ... 11
The Scourge of the Hebrews ... 52
Theobald of Chartres ... 13–4
Thessaly ... 10
Toledo ... 9, 22, 29, 35, 47, 49, 50, 55, 72, 75, 77, 78, 80, 96–7, 99, 106, 110, 111, 115, 119, 135, 137, 140
Toledo, Alfonso de ... 49
Torah ... 41

Torquemada, Juan de ... 47, 55–6, 73
Torres, Luis de ... 132n
Tortosa ... 51
Tractatus contra Madianitas et Ismaelitas ... 55
Treves ... 5
Triana, castle of ... 70–1
Tunis ... 11
Turkey ... 135, 136
Turks ... 3, 48

Valencia ... 35–7, 38, 40–1, 48, 72, 81, 85, 99, 110, 132n, 134, 140, 141
Valladolid ... 65, 73
Valladolid, Alfonso de ... 50
Venice ... 77, 134, 135, 136
Verdun ... 7
Vienna ... 7, 9
Villada, Pedro de ... 118–9, 121ff.
Vives, Miguel, the seer ... 141
voodoo ... 10–11

William of Norwich ... 13
witchcraft ... 84
Worms ... 5, 9
Wurzburg ... 8

York ... 6

Zamora ... 28
Zeal of Christ against the Jews, Saracens and Infidels ... 52
Zeus ... 10
Zola, Emile ... 77n